# A Survival Kit for Writing English
## Second Edition

It is the mark of an educated man to look for
precision in each class of things just so far as the
nature of the subject admits.
— Aristotle, *Nicomachean Ethics*

# A Survival Kit for Writing English

## Second Edition

R.F. Bailey
**School of English**
**Western Australian Institute**
**of Technology**

Longman Cheshire

Longman Cheshire Pty Limited
Longman House
Kings Gardens
95 Coventry Street
Melbourne 3205 Australia

Offices in Sydney, Brisbane, Adelaide
and Perth. Associated companies, branches,
and representatives throughout the world

First published 1976
Reprinted 1977, 1981
Second edition 1984
Reprinted 1985, 1986

Produced by Longman Cheshire Pty Limited
Printed in Hong Kong

National Library of Australia
Cataloguing-in-Publication data

Bailey, R. F. (Ray F.).
A Survival Kit for Writing English.

2nd ed.
Previous ed.: Hawthorn, Vic.: Longman Australia, 1976.
ISBN 0 582 66550 7.

1. English language — Rhetoric. 2. English language —
Style. I. Title.

808'.042

# Acknowledgements

Acknowledgment is due to the University of Chicago Press for permission to use extracts from *A Manual for Writers of Term Papers, Theses, and Dissertations* by Kate L. Turabian. I am also grateful to Penguin Books for permitting me to use extracts from George Steiner's *Language and Silence* and Denis McQuail's *Sociology of Mass Communication*, to *The Journal of Abnormal and Social Psychology* for a paragraph from Stanley Milgram's 'A Study of Obedience', and to Harper and Row for a paragraph from Jacob Bronowski's *Science and Human Values*.

I wish to record my thanks to certain of my colleagues in the School of English at the Western Australian Institute of Technology. Notable among these are Mrs A. Bollard, Dr D. Buchbinder, Dr B. H. Milech, and Dr D. I. Yeats, who gave up time to offer advice and criticism — and then stood uncomplainingly by if I perversely went my own way. I also want to thank Dr Eamon Murphy (WAIT's School of Social Sciences) for his suggestions, and Ed Lacy for permission to ransack one of his undergraduate essays for use in Chapter 4.

I wish I were able to blame someone else for any faults in the book, but the facts are blatantly otherwise; and the errors which almost inevitably remain must belong, immortally, to me.

R.F.B.

For LIZ

Who still hasn't the slightest need for it

# Preface to the Second Edition

The steady demand for this book is naturally gratifying. On the other hand, while it has clearly filled a need, the continuing presence of that need is no reason for congratulation. Students are still leaving school without what many teachers consider an adequate level of literacy, whether literacy is defined in the context of the workplace or the university. The *Survival Kit* aims to be a self-reference text for those people, whose purchase of the book shows an admirable willingness to improve themselves in some of the fundamental matters of grammar, sentence shaping, and punctuation.

Yet I never intended the book to be completely self-referential. One's improvement in any endeavour is to some extent dependent on the quality of advice received from a skilled instructor. That is one reason why I have not provided answers to the exercises, except to the Self-Test in Chapter 10; I preferred to assume the benign presence of a guiding hand, a form of supervision which will help the student realise that there can be more than one answer to the problems posed. This matters greatly. A sentence or a paragraph can be written correctly in several different ways, but its meaning can alter quite markedly depending on how it is phrased or punctuated. The notion of correctness, therefore, is not a matter of rigidity but of selection, and that is why this book encourages the application of informed common sense rather than a blind reliance on rules and regulations.

The second edition of *Survival Kit* contains a new chapter on how to write essays and paragraphs. The omission of the latter in the first edition was not an oversight;

I felt at the time that the subject was too large to admit of the simplified treatment I could give to the rest of the book, and was in some conflict with the quick, sometimes breathless discussion that seemed appropriate to such a small volume. With supervision, however, I think the new chapter will be helpful to students and others who come to grief when they have to write an efficient, high-quality essay. In this respect, the inclusion of parts of an essay written by one of my own students should not only demonstrate how a good essay might be written, but also stimulate confidence that where one student has so ably travelled, others may easily follow.

R.F.B.
Perth, Western Australia
August 1983

# Preface

Survival as an undergraduate depends, amongst many other things, on the way you impress your tutor. No one can help you very much with the content of the assignments you turn in to him, but the *Survival Kit* will at least offer positive help in expressing your thoughts forcefully as well as correctly, and in presenting the finished, proofread sheets of paper with something of a professional flourish. Even the best products look better with a little window-dressing. I mean the book to be readable as well as effective, and I mean it to be read by the matriculating high school student and the undergraduate.

There are a lot of people now who believe that the only good grammarian is a dead one. This belief has even spread to the schools, some of which have all but banned the teaching of grammar in favour of creativity and self-expression. I too am in favour of self-expression, but I don't see that it comes any better for *not* knowing grammar. Such a belief opens the dam gates to this sort of thing:

> Kippling and the playwrites of his day were writting at a time when the sun was still shinning over the British Empire.

One wonders whether 'kippling' means a drinking bout until one realises that anyone who can wreak such havoc with 'playwrights' and 'writing' is effortlessly capable of misspelling Kipling's name. And the idea of a sun which shins over the British Empire can only come from an imaginative mind or a careless one. The trouble is that we can no longer always be sure which is which. If this is the fruit of self-expression without grammar, then one can only hope that it is not quite what was intended.

Nevertheless, the day of traditional Latin-based grammar — of the subjunctive, the ablative absolute, and the noun complement — appears to be on the wane. Unfortunately, nothing satisfactory has yet appeared to replace it. What is needed, at least in the meantime, is a streamlined grammar: one that supplies certain major requirements without needing to develop into a full-scale study of its own. That is why the *Survival Kit* ignores the many terms of traditional grammar and forges two new tools of its own; the flexibility of control units and support units (especially in Chapters 2 and 3) is based purely on the meaning as intended by the writer and understood by the reader. The two new terms follow in the path of the old, since that is still the only satisfactory path there is, but the twists and turns have been straightened out and the way ahead is clearer. My desire for simple clarity has also led me away from such matters as pitch, endurance, and silence, which ought properly to have taken their places alongside intonation in Chapter 1.

The purpose of grammar is after all not to produce grammarians but to help people understand language; and the relatively simple explanations in the following pages will, I hope, achieve faster understanding than the comprehensive but intricate ones they are meant to replace.

R.F.B.
Perth, Western Australia
August 1975

# Contents

# 1 'English as She Is Spoke'

One of the first mistakes you can make about written
English is to assume that it is necessarily the same as
spoken English. This is a popular trap, perhaps because it is
frequently baited with an enticing truism: that good writing
should be as close as possible to good speech. No one
disputes the truism; unspeakable writing is bad —
unspeakably bad.. But once the truism is swallowed, the trap
is ready to be sprung, and you must take the next step with
great care. If you now say that you write the way you
speak, you may be lost. You have probably failed to
recognise that writing and speaking are two quite distinct
activities, and that what is true for one isn't necessarily true
for the other.

The purpose of good English is, of course, the same for
the pen as it is for the voice. It is to put an idea from one
mind as clearly as possible into another. Not only is it
possible to understand good English; it should be *im*possible
to *mis*understand it. Unfortunately, this is too often where
the pen and the voice part company, because although
handling the spoken word competently becomes second
nature to us, shaping the written word to our purpose is a
process which is taught, practised, and understood far less
than it should be. This is as true in its way for the English
undergraduate as it is for anyone else, and it is the reason
why this book has been written.

Some of the differences between voice and pen need to
be pointed out. To begin with, the spoken word is by
definition short-lived. It is conceived, delivered, lingers
briefly on the ear, and is gone. Like the cinema and the
television, it is a moving medium, and keeping a finger on

all the pulses from beginning to end requires either elaborate electronic assistance or the kind of memory most of us don't have. That is why a lecture or talk can be more elusive than an essay or a column in a magazine, and it is why we take more care in written work than we do in spontaneous speech. The written word is born more slowly, and printed errors have a nasty habit of outliving the person who enshrined them in type. Writing gives us a chance to examine our thoughts and words and arguments before we present them to a reader. The reader, knowing this, will judge us harshly. Care in writing, therefore, is partly a matter of sheer survival; print condemns us for the same error which, in speech, might even go unnoticed.

A sentence which is quite clear when spoken is often not at all clear in writing, as anyone will tell you who has tried to make an exact written record of a more or less spontaneous speech. Writing cannot gesticulate, grin, scowl, show its teeth, mutter under its breath, waggle its eyebrows, wink, or stamp its feet. These are the assets of the speaker, not the writer. The speaker can raise or lower his voice, can stress or subdue his pronunciation; meaning in speech, after the right words have been chosen, is largely a matter of *intonation*. It is possible, if nonsensical, to *intone* the same sentence differently in as many ways as there are words in it. Intonation is 'English as she is spoke', and it has been the basis of more than one advertising slogan. The following fictional example will demonstrate this facility.

Smith's Pills Cure Headaches *Instantly*!
Smith's Pills Cure *Headaches* Instantly!
Smith's Pills *Cure* Headaches Instantly!
Smith's *Pills* Cure Headaches Instantly!
*Smith's* Pills Cure Headaches Instantly!

The meaning alters with each change in intonation. The alterations are artificial, of course, and perhaps only the first version has any naturalness about it; that's why the printer must use *italic* type — to emphasise a word that the sentence rhythm would otherwise subdue. Italics are the most obvious device for intoning the written word. In the same way, capital letters are sometimes used to point up an important word, such as a person's name. But such systems are crude. Italic type is heavy-handed, and it can leave us *wondering why it was used*. And We Do Not Usually Speak in Capital Letters.

Something more is needed to give the written language a kind of intonation — something more subtle. It is the change of intonation (usually, delicate changes in the rise and fall and pause of the voice) which gives English speech its characteristic way of showing meaning. The problem lies in transferring this tone, this meaning, to our writing. Short of making our written words slither through a system of musical notation, there is no comprehensive way of doing it. But there is a good way, and it is called punctuation.

## Intonation and Punctuation

Spoken meaning depends on intonation; written meaning depends on punctuation. The factor common to both is meaning. Commas and full stops (and the rest) are part of the scaffolding of writing, the nuts and bolts of intonation and meaning, and they make sure that our meaning is understood — and that it is not misunderstood. Even the space between words is a form of punctuation: it separates one item of meaning from another. The system of punctuation is an imperfect thing, but it works well enough; and nobody has yet thought of a more convenient one.

This is a good time to take an old wives' tale and strangle it. There seems to be a common belief that punctuation marks are breathing pauses — that you drop a comma into your sentences whenever you think you've gone on long enough for your reader to get mentally out of breath. There may often be some truth in this, but the tail is wagging the dog. If it were completely true, then a fast speaker would use nothing except occasional commas; a slow one, full stops. Result: anarchy.

Punctuation frequently does imply a pause, but the pause is merely a useful side effect. The space between two words doesn't usually imply any sort of pause at all, yet that space is a punctuation mark. The real purpose of punctuation is to point out a separation of meaning. Look at this example:

Let's eat, Harry!

That seems clear enough: we're inviting Harry to share a meal with us. Now see the same words without the comma:

Let's eat Harry!

Again the meaning is clear. Harry has arrived among cannibals.

No normal speaker will say either of those sentences with any significant pause between words (comma or no comma) and still sound normal. Yet that tiny tadpole of a comma is enough to change the whole meaning of the sentence — because it represents a change in *intonation*. Harry's hospitable friends drop their voices a little when they come to his name; his cannibalistic cronies say all three words in the same tone. The comma creates this difference between them without making any sort of breathing pause at all. This is the main reason, by the way, why we punctuate on both sides of any form of address, i.e., any name which is used in a sentence to talk *to* a person rather than *about* him.

Now let's see an example of a sentence in which a comma makes a difference in meaning *and* creates a pause. This one was taken from an Australian daily newspaper:

Mr Frank Drake-Brown, peanut farmer, president of the State P & C Association and Premier of Northland, today opened a new school.

That, at any rate is what the sentence presumably should have been. This is how it actually appeared:

Mr Frank Drake-Brown, peanut, farmer, president of the State P & C Association and Premier of Northland, today opened a new school.

Needless to say, essential names have been changed. Knowing that the Australian colloquialism 'peanut' means 'nitwit', we can see only two possibilities: the sentence was composed by a person who didn't understand punctuation, or by a person who understood it very well and had a decided political opinion. That comma creates a pause in meaning, and any pause in time is irrelevant.

As that example shows, you can't distinguish between the information you write about and the punctuation that goes with it. Usually, the two things are the same. To drive the point home, here is a further example, this time taken from an Australian Sunday newspaper:

> This week we interviewed a 22-year-old Perth housewife, a deserted mother, with a young son who has taken up the oldest profession in the world.

No public outcry seems to have followed this scandalous revelation about the wretched child, so we must suppose that it is the mother who turned to prostitution, not the boy, and that the purple comma should come after 'son', not 'mother'. Perhaps both these last examples will give you a clue about why some lawyers regard commas with nearly apoplectic horror; they should certainly convince you of the importance punctuation has for meaning.

Punctuation, and particularly the middle stop (see Chapters 2, 3 and 5), separates one meaning from another. If a sentence is built on only one meaning, no middle stop is necessary; if it is built on more than one meaning, then at least one middle stop is probably vital. These individual 'meanings' are called **control units** or **support units** in this book, and the next two chapters explain them more fully and tell you how to use them.

Some may object here that the context of the sentence will prevent misinterpretations of the kind we have been looking at. This is simple-minded. Even if it were always true, which it isn't, it wouldn't prevent the possibility of misinterpretation; and only a bad writer will willingly permit such a possibility in his writing. It just isn't good enough to say that speech and writing are adequate if they can be understood. Most people would understand the heading of this chapter ('English as She Is Spoke'), but they wouldn't say it is good English. 'Bill done that' is just as understandable. So is the South Sea Islander's way of talking of a missionary helicopter as a Mixmaster-Him-Belong-Jesus-Christ. Quaint, perhaps, but it hardly represents a desirable norm. If this is acceptable English, what is unacceptable? Wee mite az wel rite owr langwij fernetikli an hav dun with the hole biznes.

The fashionable word in this context is 'communication', and it needs watching. We are told that the important thing is to 'communicate', and this is such an obvious remark that we elevate it to the status of godhead and worship it as an all-embracing truth. Relevant here is a remark made by Sir Ernest Gowers in a speech to the English Association in London in 1957:

> The revolt against the old grammarians seems to be producing a school of thought who hold that grammar is obsolete and it does not matter how we write so long as we can make ourselves understood. It cannot be denied that if we had to choose between the two, it would be better to be ungrammatical than unintelligible. But we do not have to choose between the two. We can rid ourselves of those grammarians' fetishes which make it more difficult to be intelligible without throwing the baby away with the bath water.

Writing good English is a job requiring common sense and moderation. Infanticides need not apply.

Beware of the word 'communication'. It is a noble word which has been devalued by overuse and lends itself too readily to the computer terminology of some Business English books. Speaking, these books tell us, is 'encoding a message', and listening is 'decoding a message'. Nobody seems to 'talk' or 'listen' any more; electronic phraseology sounds so much more important. Like all jargon, such terminology isn't irritating provided it serves a useful purpose; but it is often unnecessary, and at worst it takes attention away from some of the finer details of writing — details which have such a vital bearing on the clarity and sense of the written sentence.

A final word. Punctuation is used according to meaning rather than to please grammarians. But remember that grammar is merely a series of observations about language, designed to point the way to sensible, clear usage. If the grammarian is any good, then his rules go hand in hand with common sense — and ultimately common sense and the rules are one and the same thing.

## Exercise 1

1 Turn back to those five sentences about Smith's Pills on page 2. What is the meaning of each of the five versions?
2 Look at the 'Let's eat Harry' examples. Remember the need to punctuate before and after a form of address.

Then write out the following sentences, punctuating any forms of address you can find and pointing out any ambiguities.

(a) Hello men!
(b) Are you coming to see Joan?
(c) I know Harry well.
(d) Put the kettle on Montague.
(e) Won't you come in Ichabod?
(f) Welcome Miss Entwhistle.
(g) If I really wanted to cut you down to size you idiot, I'd have to dig a hole first.

# 2 The Powerhouse Sentence

To have any meaning at all, the English language relies heavily on its word order. We don't say 'Cat the off put switch out light the and'. We say 'Put the cat out and switch off the light' — or, if we live in an unusual household, 'Put the light out and switch off the cat'. It is all a question of word order. There is a world of difference between 'Bill hit Joe' and 'Joe hit Bill', especially to Bill and Joe. Only word order stands between victory and a black eye.

And the word order stays the same in the majority of English sentences. This is it:

| Subject group | Verb group |
|---|---|
| Bill | hit Joe. |

A subject group is followed by a verb group. These two groups added together make a **control unit**; they make up one complete word group ('unit' comes from the Latin word *unus*, which means 'one'), and that word group controls everything else that happens in the sentence. Other word groups can be added to the sentence, all supporting the meaning of the control unit by adding more meanings to it. These word groups are called **support units**, and they are helpless without a control unit. Here is a support unit masquerading as a sentence:

Rising and falling as they went.

It is aimless. It is a poor, empty fragment of meaning; it is a sentence fragment. Add a control unit and the picture is a different one:

Rising and falling as they went, **the horses slowly swam across the river**.

Adding a control unit (printed here in **bold type**) rescues the support unit from meaningless oblivion. In other words, a control unit shapes a purposeful meaning out of blind chaos: it creates a sentence.

Recognising a control unit is easy. You simply recognise which part of the sentence carries the main meaning and controls the other parts. This means that you must recognise the main point the writer is making in his sentence, which you can already do. If you sometimes have difficulty recognising this, then either the sentence has not been well made or the reader has not read it properly. Once you know where the control unit is, it becomes easy knowing where punctuation must go; and this knowledge, as Chapter 1 tried to show, is often crucial to prevent misinterpretation.

## The Control Unit

No sentence is a sentence without a control unit. And a control unit is not a control unit unless it has two parts: a subject which controls everything else in the sentence, and a verb under the direct rule of the subject. The following control unit is usually regarded as being the shortest sentence in the Bible:

**Jesus wept**.

A subject, remember, is a person, group or thing which does something ('Jesus'), and a verb is a word or words telling us what the subject is up to ('wept'). The fact that a control unit can also be a sentence shows its power; it can claim a full stop at any time and become a sentence in its own right. This happens a lot, and such sentences needn't be as short as 'Jesus wept'. Both the subject and the verb can have more than one word:

| Subject group | Verb group |
| --- | --- |
| **The aircraft** | **is landing.** |
| **Mike and Freda** | **started to laugh.** |
| **The man in the stocks** | **was beginning to shout.** |

This is why it is more accurate to say that a control unit consists of subject and verb *groups*. Here is a longer example of a sentence which is all one control unit:

**My brother's first examinations at his new school began the day he arrived there.**

All the words in that sentence seem to be vital. If you try to reduce the sentence to the absolutely basic subject and verb, you will get 'My brother's examinations began'. This is all right, but you've lost something. The whole point of the sentence is that the examinations were the boy's first at the new school and that they began almost before he'd had time to draw breath. All the words are therefore parts of the same single meaning, the same unit (remember that a unit involves a concept of one-ness), and the entire sentence is therefore one complete control unit. There are no support units anywhere in sight — and therefore no commas, semicolons, colons, dashes, or brackets.

That last point is crucial. Since a control unit is *one* meaning, there should be no middle stops (commas, etc.) to break it up; middle stops are used almost exclusively to separate a control unit from support units, or to separate one support unit from another. They are not used to break up a unit on its own. For example, you wouldn't use middle stops here:

Wrong

**Jesus, wept.**
**Bill, kicked, Harry.**
**The car went; down the street.**

The middle stops are wrong: punctuation should never be used to separate the inseparable.

There are only two exceptions to this rule. You are quite familiar with the first, which directs that one adjective is separated from another with a comma. This is true whether the adjectives fall into the subject group or the verb group:

**The cheerful, casual manner was a fake.**
**The careful, intricate, detailed plan went wrong.**
**He was a friendly, happy companion.**
**Prentice turned to his tall, dark, silent host.**

So the only reason for using *single* middle stops inside a control unit is to separate adjectives with a comma. The other exception to the rule is the use of a matching *pair* of middle stops, such as a pair of brackets, and involves the action of a support unit breaking into the control unit between the subject and verb groups (e.g., '**Goliath**, the Philistines' secret weapon, **terrified all of David's friends**'). Before we deal with that, however, perhaps a summary of the story so far would be useful. You will find it in Fig. 1.

*Fig. 1  The control unit*

|  |  |
| --- | --- |
| **Subject group** | **Verb group** |
| **The house** | **was burning.** |

(a) A control unit (subject group and verb group) carries your intended essential meaning in a sentence. You cannot reduce a control unit without simultaneously reducing meaning. Since a control unit is a complete single unit, you should not break it into sub-units by using middle stops.
(b) Always identify a control unit accurately. Recognising the powerhouse of your own sentences is one of the most basic, and instinctive, tasks of an organised writer's mind. Failure to recognise it may lead to a chaos of misunderstanding.
(c) Both the subject and verb groups can hold several words:

> **Running up and down a ladder can become a terrible strain on the legs.**

(d) Use middle stops inside a control unit only when separating adjectives with commas, and when using matching pairs of middle stops around a support unit which intrudes between the subject and verb.

# Support Units

The control unit carries your essential meaning, but a skeleton is a little grisly without flesh and blood. Adding other word groups to a control unit can help to bring the sentence to life. These other word groups are controlled by the control unit, for they have no independent subject and verb groups of their own. To remind you that a support unit cannot exist on its own, here is a very lonely example:

Although it was cold.

It is a sentence fragment. There is no action because there is no control unit. Once a control unit is added, meaning becomes complete:

Although it was cold, **I didn't bother with a coat.**
**The sea that day,** although it was cold, **was a wonderful sight.**
**Nobody lit a fire,** although it was cold.

The words in bold type are control units. Using type in this way demonstrates the superior importance of control units, and perhaps it is a pity that we cannot use this printer's technique in our own writing. Fortunately a support unit can almost always be recognised without it: there is usually a middle stop operating between support and control, and sometimes a support is introduced by a tell-tale announcing word. Such a word is 'although', and it is used in the three previous examples. Notice that an announcing word can reduce a control unit to a support unit:

**It was cold.** (*Control unit*)
Although it was cold. (*Support unit*)
**I struggled furiously.** (*Control unit*)
When I struggled furiously. (*Support unit*)

As you see, that announcing word is a real give-away. It gives you the unmistakable signal that the word group it belongs to is a support unit, and you know that a control unit must be lurking somewhere about. There is one trap you can fall into, but it is a very obvious one:

When I work, **I have to be in the right mood.**
(*Support unit and control unit*)
**When I work depends on how I feel.**
(*Control unit alone*)

In that second example, 'When I work' is not a support unit — it is the subject group of the control unit, and it must not be separated from its verb group by a middle stop.

If you will pardon a brief digression, there is another point we can deal with in passing. The sentence fragment (i.e., a support unit on its own) is an incomplete sentence, an incomplete thought, and should therefore be avoided. But there is an occasion when its use can be justified; it is a conversational device, and we all use it in everyday speech:

*Interviewer*: **When did you realise you'd been burgled**, Miss Peep?
*Bo Peep*: When I went to the sheep-fold next morning.

Miss Peep's reply is a sentence fragment, a standard feature of dialogue, and it relies totally on the existence of a previous full sentence. If you are writing dialogue, feel free to use the device; otherwise, make sure that all your sentences really are sentences, and leave sentence fragments to conversational stylists.

Now, back to those three sentences we looked at earlier. Here they are again, and they illustrate the fact that a middle stop separates a support unit from a control unit, and also that a support unit can be put into a sentence in any of three places — before the control, after it, or inside it between the subject and verb groups:

| Support unit | Control unit | |
|---|---|---|
| Although it was cold, | **I didn't bother with a coat.** | |

| Control unit | Support unit | |
|---|---|---|
| **Nobody lit a fire,** | although it was cold. | |

| Subject group | Support unit | Verb group |
|---|---|---|
| **The sea that day,** | although it was cold, | **was a wonderful sight.** |

Follow this rule: where one unit touches another, punctuate. The almost invariable stop is the comma. In the case of a support unit placed in the middle position (between the subject group and the verb group), be very sure to punctuate fore and aft — at *both* ends of the support. Failure to do so lets the middle support unit collide with either the subject group or the verb group, perhaps causing a few seconds of chaos for your reader. Punctuating fore and aft around a middle support is the concept of matching *pairs* of middle stops, and it is the second of those two exceptions to the rule about not punctuating inside a control unit. With middle supports, be sure to use only one of three kinds of middle stop: a pair of commas (,,), a pair of brackets ( ( ) ), or a pair of dashes (— —). Which pair you use depends on the emphasis you want, and we shall look at that soon. For the moment, though, we shall move more slowly and examine, one by one, those three positions where a support unit may join a sentence.

## Support Units Placed First

> To tell you the truth, **I couldn't care less.**
> His army shattered, **Hannibal fled into hiding.**
> At dawn on the day appointed, **the four of us met secretly.**

Beginning a sentence with a support unit suspends the action; you have to wait for the control unit to come along. This device lets you do a little scene-setting, perhaps to conjure up some atmosphere before you swing into action with your control unit. Use a middle stop (almost always a comma) to keep the two units from colliding; apart from being logical, a comma throws some emphasis onto both units by making your reader pause for a fleeting moment while he adjusts to the balance of your meanings. The comma is the usual middle stop between units, but you might occasionally want to use the dash — which breaks up the flow of words so that your reader can't help feeling the emphasis. Be sparing with the dash, though; it has about as much subtlety as a four-inch naval gun, and your sentence had better be worthy of the punch it gives.

These are the only two middle stops you will use between a control unit and a support unit placed first. Sometimes you may not need to use any middle stop at all; this

14

happens when the separate meanings of the two units are quite clear and do not need to be emphasised —

If you're late **you can find your own way home.**

— or when the sentence as a whole would be over-punctuated if you used a stop there:

When twelve o'clock came **the drink ran out**, closely followed by the drinkers.

Although strictly logical, a comma before 'the drink ran out' gets the reader tangled up in the next comma, so that the sentence jerks and bumps disconcertingly. But be careful before you decide to omit commas between units in case you cause a head-on collision:

Wrong
**His army shattered Hannibal fled into hiding**.

At first sight it appears that poor Hannibal was set upon by a thousand men. The comma after 'shattered' must be restored.

Another diagram might help. The purple triangle indicates that the comma should be used, but that it can be omitted under the circumstances already described:

| First support | △ | Control unit |
|---|---|---|

The next day **we left for Yokohama.**

# Middle Support Units

| Subject group | Middle support | Verb group |
|---|---|---|

**The new nurse**, a very efficient girl, **found herself in demand.**
**Only the proofreading** (a boring job) **remained to him.**
**My new job** — the third in a year — **looks interesting.**

Using a middle support (one which comes between the subject group and the verb group) is the grammatical equivalent of a breaking-and-entering job. The control unit is forced open so that the intruding support unit can tell your reader more about the subject. Any support unit has a meaning which is separate from other units, and this separateness must be protected. A support unit placed first throws out a comma guard before the oncoming control unit; a support unit placed last posts a similar guard after the preceding control unit; and a middle support uses a matching pair of stops on either side, to separate itself from the preceding subject group and the following verb group. When you use a middle support you have a choice of three pairs of stops: a comma pair, a bracket pair, and a dash pair. Each pair has a special effect on the reader. A comma pair barely slows him down, and makes him read your middle support almost on equal terms with your control unit; a bracket pair softens the interruption so that he barely notices it and tends to skip over it; and a dash pair breaks open the control unit with such force that the middle support comes rippling off the page and shouts its importance to the world.

**The old mansion,** our family's home since 1758, **was on fire.**
**The old mansion** (you'll remember it well) **is still burning.**
**The old mansion** — scene of countless debaucheries — **was burning furiously.**

Remember that a middle support always requires a pair of middle stops. If it isn't a pair, think how daft it'll look. Suppose I were to use only the second half of a bracket pair, like this?) You'd have to go chasing back along the sentence, looking for its mate. (Or suppose I were to use only the first half, like that?

Forgetting one half of a pair of commas or dashes is just as serious. A bracket mistake is more obvious only because you're used to thinking of brackets in pairs, and of commas and dashes as single stops. Here's another example of a middle support properly separated with a comma pair:

**Dr Doe,** my wife's brother, **came to dinner last night.**

Now see what happens when one of the commas is missed out:

**Dr Doe,** my wife's brother came to dinner last night.

The sentence is turned into a speech, and a new control unit is created. The words are the same, but the meaning has changed: we are now telling Dr Doe what happened the night before.

An equally common mistake is to put the comma-pair in where it is not wanted. A middle support always needs it, but sometimes the writer thinks he sees a middle support when one isn't there. Always check that what you think is a middle support is not a vital part of the subject group:

Wrong

**Ships**, which are going to sink, **should be avoided.**

The comma pair is wrong. A middle support unit can be taken out of the sentence without damage to the writer's meaning. Applying this test to the example, we get this:

Wrong

**Ships should be avoided.**

This is absurd: it is certainly not what was meant. 'Which are going to sink' is essential to 'ships', and the whole lot is one subject group. No commas are allowed:

**Ships which are going to sink should be avoided.**

Now I'm saying that you should avoid any ship which looks as if it might not be seaworthy. The whole sentence is one control unit, which carries no internal middle stops because its meaning is *one* meaning. If you are ever in doubt about whether you've written a long subject group or a middle support unit, try mentally putting a bracket pair around the words under suspicion. If the meaning of the sentence outside the brackets is still the same meaning you intended, then the words you've mentally bracketed are obviously a separate word group — a middle support unit — and should be protected against the control unit on both sides with the appropriate pair of matching middle stops. If the meaning of the sentence outside the brackets is not the same meaning you intended, then your mental brackets have obviously mauled the subject group, and a matching pair of middle stops must not be used.

# Support Units Placed Last

Finally, a support unit can enter a sentence after the control unit. In the next diagram, the purple triangle is again used to indicate that a separating comma should be used, but that it can be omitted for reasons very similar to the ones described in 'Support units placed first'.

---

Control unit △ Support unit

---

(a) **Mycroft's mechanic gets bonuses**, sometimes twice a week.
(b) **Mycroft's mechanic gets bonuses** — but not time off.
(c) **Mycroft's mechanic gets bonuses** (especially in winter).
(d) **Mycroft's mechanic gets bonuses** as well as a wage.

---

A support unit placed last is very similar to one placed first — you choose your separating stop according to the amount of separation needed. With a first support, remember, you can choose to separate with a comma, a dash (rarely), or perhaps no stop at all; with a last support, this range of choice is exactly the same but with the additional option of a pair of brackets. If we ask a series of questions about the four examples above, the choice of separating stops should be made clear.

(a) Q. What does Mycroft's mechanic get?
    A. **Bonuses,** and sometimes twice a week.
       (*The casual effect of a comma*)
(b) Q. What does Mycroft's mechanic get?
    A. **Bonuses.** But the poor chap gets no time off!
       (*The punch of a dash*)
(c) Q. What does Mycroft's mechanic get?
    A. **Bonuses.** Incidentally, though, he only gets them really when he works outside in winter.
       (*The subduing effect of brackets*)
(d) Q. What does Mycroft's mechanic get?
    A. **Bonuses as well as a wage.**
       (*Leaving out a stop lets a word of the support unit become a part of the verb group*)

The tone of the answers should explain the particular middle stop used (or not used) in each case. (a) answers the question and adds extra information; the two meanings on either side of the comma are therefore separate but almost equally important. (b) answers the question but adds important extra information. (This calls for a stronger mark than the comma: never send a boy to do a man's job.) (c) adds a fairly unimportant detail to the answer, and tones down the importance with a bracket pair.* The use of brackets in this position is rare, by the way; you can almost always get away with a comma or perhaps a dash.

The fourth example (d) is a bit of a cheat, of course. There isn't really a final support unit at all — just a long verb group. The sentence means that it's just as important to know that the mechanic gets a wage as it is to know that he gets bonuses. Therefore, no separation of meaning; therefore again, no comma. Judging when to punctuate before a final support unit means judging the subtle nuances of your intended meanings. If there are no nuances, there is no punctuation. If in doubt, try mentally putting a dash before the suspect support unit: if it works, then you've got a case for a comma, and perhaps the dash itself if you want a bold effect.

## Support Units In All Three Positions

Obviously, you are not restricted to one support at a time. You can use supports in all three positions at once if you wish, and you can even use more than one support in the same position. The following diagram uses purple circles to indicate a compulsory pair of matching middle stops, and purple triangles where a middle stop is usually advisable but sometimes unnecessary.

You can use as many support units as you think are necessary, but make sure you keep your sentence smooth and flowing, and don't obscure the control unit. Remember to punctuate always around a middle support, and always in other places where not to do so might cause misreading. In the first example, for instance, the comma after 'smashed' is necessary to prevent this confusion:

---

* Notice that the full stop here goes outside the brackets. See the later section on brackets for a discussion of this point.

Wrong

**Their hopes smashed the South African and his friends.**

In the second example, there is no comma after 'night'. Using a comma there would be using one comma too many; the sentence would find itself plagued with a swarm of wriggling tadpoles through which the meaning would barely trickle. Always exercise discretion, for too much punctuation is almost as bad as too little.

| First Support | △ | Subject Group | ○ | Middle Support | ○ | Verb Group | △ | Last Support |
|---|---|---|---|---|---|---|---|---|

Their hopes smashed, **the South African and his friends**, including Jo-Jo's nephew, **fled to the sea** away from the menace in the east.

In the dead of night **the company's helicopter**, which had been parked two hundred metres from the bush hotel, **burst into flame** in the most spectacular conflagration since November the Fifth.

Since my main competitor had fallen ill, and knowing that the job vacancy had to be filled quickly, **I knew my chances of promotion were better now than they had ever been in the last five years**, in spite of my speech impediment, my wooden leg, and my hatred of the boss.

One final point. The first two sentences in that last diagram do not use commas before the last support unit, preferring an almost invisible under-punctuation to a jarring, jerky over-correctness. Remember that a final support unit chooses to ignore its rightful comma far more frequently than a first support does, thereby quietly allowing the final support to become a part of the verb group. This is a habit you will find easy to adopt, but it increases your responsibility to your reader in making sure that there is no possibility whatsoever of a misreading.

# Exercise 2

Write out the following sentences, putting a wavy line under the control units and adding suitable punctuation. If any of the sentences are fragments, say so — then write out your suggested alteration. Point out any sentence which is already correct.

1 Motorists who drive badly are dangerous.
2 I always thought a sextant which is really a ship's navigational instrument was a naval pervert.
3 Because I really want to be a motor mechanic teaching me good English is about as useful as teaching a polar bear how to catch a kangaroo.
4 Judging by the way he insulted Oscar Beardsley's eventual expulsion from Wilde's circle was inevitable.
5 Learning French because you might one day visit France makes as much sense as building a dug-out canoe because you might sometime sail up the Orinoco.
6 Underestimating your opponent can be fatal.
7 Chappell side-stepped the ball clipping it smartly to the boundary as he did so.
8 John called to his sister who then came to join us.
9 Now back to those three sentences we looked at earlier.
10 The worst disease of man old age has few compensations.

## Exercise 3

The following sentences are wrongly punctuated. The marks printed in purple are a broad hint. Rewrite each sentence correctly and describe the fault.

1 The fire he and his men had struggled with for so long, was at last dying down.
2 Isaac Newton, often called the Father of Modern Physics left Cambridge when the plague closed in.
3 You should read *1984* — it is available in paperback, before you tackle *The Wanting Seed*.
4 Studies, of his latest novel, show a growing critical interest in his work.
5 The committee's plans, were approved by the council.
6 People (who are dishonest) should be punished.
7 'Pon my honour sir, I swear you were born to hang.
8 Carlyle said that the true university of his day, was a collection of books.

9 The Press always reports the events, of the Prime
  Minister's overseas trips.
10 People who listen to Mr Thespis, and the only advantage
  in listening to him in the first place is to discover that
  there is no reason to listen to him again — have found
  as good a way of wasting time as any yet devised.

## End Note

One of the tricks of the writing trade is a handy little device
known as parallelism. Of the several ways of learning this
trick, perhaps the most appropriate to Chapter 2 are best
approached along two avenues: the matching pair of stops,
and the hinged series of stops. Used with discretion, they
will add power to your elbow.

### The Matching Pair

The middle support unit discussed in this chapter comes, as
you know, between the subject and verb groups. It needs a
pair of middle stops to surround it inside the control unit,
and therefore demands exemption from the control unit's
general ban on middle stops. We can now take the matter
further by saying that a support unit can be added to a
sentence *inside* another support unit, or inside the control
unit's subject group or verb group. To put it another way,
you can have a middle support unit that isn't in the middle.
In the following remark by Sir Winston Churchill about a
political rival, a support unit just like this pops up right in
the middle of the verb group:

> **We know that he has**, more than any other man, **the gift of
> compressing the largest amount of words into the smallest
> amount of thought.**

That interruptive support unit doesn't come between the
subject and verb groups, but it does come in the middle of
the verb group. In a sense, therefore, it is still a middle
support and should be treated like one: with a matching
pair of middle stops. This is a common feature of English
sentences; you will find it in the first sentence of this section
('The middle . . . verb groups.').

You can put this feature to work in the subject group, too, where it looks just like an ordinary middle support. But it is really a second subject group, generated by the first one to swell its own impact:

**One more indignity**, one more outrageously intimate ransacking of his precious privacy, **would make him fall upon his enemies like a hawk upon its prey.**

That second subject group (it needs its comma pair) makes the sentence gather weight, makes the meaning rise to a peak before plunging down into the verb group and rolling remorselessly up to its close. Doubling the subject group is like harnessing two furnaces together: do it properly and your sentence will breathe fire.

The impact of that example came partly from the repeated 'one more'. This is parallelism: the addition of a new thought which is parallel to the existing one. Here is parallelism again, this time back in the verb group:

**It would take too sudden a psychological adjustment**, a change in thinking too radical for their traditionalist minds, **to convince her audience that they must now rely on a woman they had always regarded as a political gadfly.**

The verb group is interrupted by a support unit; once more a comma pair marks the frontiers of the new recruit, and once more repetition points up the parallelism ('too sudden . . . too radical'). The device underlines the writer's opinion of her audience.

## The Hinged Series

The idea of hinged middle stops is mentioned briefly in Chapter 5 (page 62), but the part it can play in parallelism makes it relevant here.

You will very often need to make one subject group perform more than one action. The most elementary way of doing this is to repeat the subject group as many times as there are actions — in other words, to write a sentence each time:

**They came running. They came jumping.**

But you cannot take this to excess without putting some

readers to sleep and driving the rest mad. The next most elementary solution is to join the two verb groups with 'and' and control them both with the same subject group:

**They came running and jumping.**

This gives you one verb group. This tactic is not recommended, however, when more than two or three actions are needed:

**They came running and jumping and yelling and laughing and squalling and tumbling.**

Instead of that primitive repetition of 'and', let the verb group split itself apart — into several verb groups under the control of the one subject group:

**They came running, jumping, yelling and laughing, squalling and tumbling like lion cubs at play, never caring or even knowing that the sands of their childhood were fast trickling away.**

All those -*ing* verbs signal separate verb groups, controlled by the subject group 'they'. They must either be joined in the same verb group by 'and' (this happens twice for variety) or kept apart by middle stops, as if they were support units. The middle stops here are commas (don't use anything stronger), which let the sentence swing down as if on hinges, backwards and forwards in a smooth, well-oiled motion to the end of its arc. This is parallelism again, with the -*ing* repetition being stressed and reinforced by the comma-hinges. The whole sentence is a control unit (you might argue that the last verb group is a support unit, but the matter is trivial), and yet we have allowed middle stops to creep into it — purely to indicate that a control unit may control several verb groups at once, rather like a missile with multiple warheads.

Another advantage of parallelism — once again in harness with a series of comma-hinges — is the tremendous emphasis it can give. It is verbally equivalent to thumping the table or wagging a finger as you speak. Here is an example of its browbeating effect, taken from Samuel Johnson's indignant letter to Lord Chesterfield in 1755, when the nobleman had publicly praised Johnson's *Dictionary* after having previously ignored the author's request for help:

Seven years, My Lord, have now passed since I waited in your outward rooms or was repulsed from your door; during which time I have been pushing on my work through difficulties of which it is useless to complain, and have brought it at last to the verge of publication — *without one act of assistance, one word of encouragement, or one smile of favour.*\*

The repeated 'one' points up the parallelism with the help of the hingeing commas, while the spirit of 'without' whispers underneath.

This brings us to a more complex example. If you can drop a single word (such as 'without' above) then you can also drop part of a control unit. Take this control unit as a base:

**It has been delayed till I am indifferent and cannot enjoy it.**

If you wish to list more consequences of this delay, apart from the one that makes up the present control unit, you can place them as extra verb groups. Use a couple of commas to mark their independence and to hinge the series. Here now is that control unit, duly expanded; it is taken from later in Johnson's letter and is preceded by a build-up sentence. See how the verb groups strike like hammer-blows on the fact of Chesterfield's delay:

The notice which you have been pleased to take of my labours, if it had been taken earlier, would have been kind. **But it has been delayed till I am indifferent and cannot enjoy it, till I am solitary and cannot impart it, till I am known — and do not want it.**

The three verb groups all begin with 'till' and are all directly controlled by 'delayed'. They are all part of the control unit. The subject group and verb are dropped after the first time, but you know they are there; you can hear Johnson's angry growl three times through 'it has been delayed', even though he uses the words only once. This is the force of parallelism, reinforced by comma-hinges.

---

\* In this and the following example, I plead guilty to tampering with Johnson's punctuation and choice of words. I do so because I can better make my point — and his — by accepting that 220 years of change have made Johnson's eighteenth-century English less accessible to those modern readers who do not know him.

# 3 The 'Comma Fanboys' Sentence

The starting point for Chapter 2 was that every sentence has to have a control unit. The starting point for Chapter 3 is that any sentence may have as many control units as it can comfortably hold.

It shouldn't take you long to spot the contradiction here. If a control unit controls everything in the sentence, then there cannot be another control unit in the sentence, since that which controls everything cannot be controlled. Yet the sentence containing more than one control unit is the most frequent type of sentence in the language. How do we account for this apparent contradiction?

First of all, we should remind ourselves that control units (and their attendant support units) must be kept firmly apart; they are separate groups of meaning, and letting them come into direct contact means that one control unit is likely to short-circuit the other:

Wrong

**It was one of the most blatant cases of cheating Mason had ever seen the Brigadier rose very slowly from the table.**

The two control units have become fused, the first smashing headlong into the other, quite confusing the reader for a couple of vital moments. The obvious way of de-fusing these fused sentences is to drag them apart with a full stop:

**It was one of the most blatant cases of cheating Mason had ever seen. The Brigadier rose very slowly from the table.**

As we know, then, a suitable end stop (i.e., full stop, exclamation mark or question mark) is the most obvious way of separating one control unit from another. The

26

separation must be heavy, because control units are powerhouses of meaning which insist on their own separate territory; as we already use commas to separate support units (the weaker mark for the weaker unit), we obviously cannot use the same mark to separate the much stronger control units. This is what happens when a comma is used wrongly in this way:

> In the silence that had fallen, **Dr Prendergast gently picked up the suddenly lethal test tube,** holding it gingerly in one hand, moving aside to let him pass, **the three other chemists made a kind of attenuated, funereal guard of honour to the door.**

The two control units and their supports have been too weakly separated, spliced uncomfortably together with an inadequate comma, so that the reader is thrown off balance by two alien support units skirmishing in a grammatical no-man's-land. So the comma after 'hand' is too weak; we know that a full stop could easily replace it, quite properly creating two sentences, but a semicolon might work just as well:

> In the silence that had fallen, **Dr Prendergast gently picked up the suddenly lethal test tube**, holding it gingerly in one hand; moving aside to let him pass, **the three other chemists made a kind of attenuated, funereal guard of honour to the door.**

The semicolon does work. It separates the first control unit and its cluster of supports from the second control unit and support; it does so very firmly in the manner of a full stop, but it keeps both control units *in the same sentence*. This is the virtue of the semicolon — that it separates as powerfully as the full stop but without any of its aggression. Ideally, therefore, the semicolon should be used to separate two control units whose meanings are closely linked:

> **He was usually a good correspondent; he used to write at least once a week.**

The semicolon is the most suitable strong separator here, for it flashes two messages to the reader: that one control unit has finished and another is about to begin, so that technically a full stop might be used; but that the two units are linked closely enough in meaning for the full stop to be just a little too vicious in separating them.

So far, then, there have been two ways of keeping control units at arm's length from each other. The full stop is strong enough to separate control units into different sentences, and the semicolon, unlike the comma, has the weight to create what might be called sub-sentences — two control units which are distinct but nonetheless linked closely in meaning. Now we come to three other forms of 'linked separation', all of which are like the semicolon in that they signify a definite separateness without causing the sentence to come to an end. These three devices are the colon, the dash, and the 'comma fanboys' system. The first two, also like the semicolon, are treated separately in the next chapter on middle stops, so they will come in only fleetingly here. The following paragraphs will therefore devote themselves mainly to 'comma fanboys'.

'Comma fanboys' is a mnemonic, a simple memory aid, and it comes to this:

---

### The 'Comma Fanboys' System

---

| | |
|---|---|
| , for | When two or more control units and their support |
| , and | units are closely linked in meaning, join them with a |
| , nor | comma followed by the appropriate 'fanboys' word. |
| , but | Never join control units with a comma on its own. |
| , or | |
| , yet | |
| , so | |

---

When preceded by a comma, those seven words are joiners. They join two or more control units and their attendant support units in a closely meshed whole, where the separate meanings are too closely related for a full stop or even a semicolon to be appropriate. Here are examples of 'comma fanboys' in action:

> It had been a remarkable meeting, for not one of the usually violent dissenters had got angry.
>
> In no time at all the matter was decided, and there was little trouble in the War Room from then on.
>
> The disputing parties have never bothered to negotiate, nor do they seem likely to begin now.

**Professor Peabody's political opinions,** despite her discretion, **had soon become known** all over the campus of her university, but **nobody seemed to worry much about them.**

**He knew he had to finish his essay by morning,** or **his tutor was sure to be his usual tiresome self.**

**The local consumer vigilantes had not seen the advertisement,** yet **it is doubtful if any of them,** preoccupied and overworked as they were, **would have had time to do anything about it.**

**I worked non-stop all night,** so **I'll thank you to keep your 'Good morning!' to yourself.**

'Comma fanboys' is as easy as that. When you use any of those seven words to join two control units, always use a comma in front of it. The two together signal the reader that a separate, but linked, control unit is coming up.

So now there are three methods of separating control units. To see how they work together, look at the following list of control units and support units, which for the moment are presented only as sentences. As usual, the control units are printed in bold type:

1 As do all strongly held beliefs, **this myth embodies elements of truth.**
2 **It tells us more truth about those who created it than about those who still believe in it.**
3 In the modern world **it must be regarded as a vestige,** a superstition.
4 In past centuries **it was part of the spiritual life-blood of the people.**
5 Because of it, **we can steal a glimpse into the mind of the early race.**
6 **We might even learn something specific about the fears and hopes they had.**
7 **We do not necessarily learn anything about the modern mind at all.**

If they are left as sentences, these meaning groups have a dogged, jerky effect. They can be moulded together much more satisfactorily:

As do all strongly held beliefs, **this myth embodies elements of truth,** but **it tells us more truth about those who created it than about those who still believe in it.** In the modern world **it must be regarded as a vestige,** a superstition; in past centuries **it was part of the spiritual life-blood of the people.** Because of it, **we can steal a glimpse into the mind of the the early race,** and **we**

**might even learn something specific about the fears and hopes they had; but we do not necessarily learn anything about the modern mind at all.**

We have turned those seven simple sentences into three sophisticated ones. Please note — this is important — that the sophistication is not simply a matter of punctuation or 'comma fanboys', since these are mere mechanical devices. The sophistication arises from a recognition of the meaning-linkages. The first control unit makes a statement, and the second instantly modifies its meaning. The two must therefore be taken together as a single meaning, a single sentence, and that is the force of the , but used to make the link. The next two control units are two aspects of the same thing — one dealing with the past and the other with the present, in a continuation of the second control unit — and the semicolon is the ideal connection for them. Then we get to 'steal a glimpse', to gain a general impression — more than that, we might actually 'learn something specific'; the one is a direct development of the other, and the , and builds the bridge between the two. The final semicolon, however, introduces a new note, for a comma would have done an adequate job in a standard 'comma fanboys' operation. The semicolon is used because a comma has already been used twice very recently in the sentence, and because the last control unit is so placed that it catches up the main threads of the paragraph and firmly reiterates the main point of the first sentence. Because the last control unit has such impact, its separation by a semicolon is justified. This is therefore a refinement of 'comma fanboys', which can become 'semicolon fanboys' under those two circumstances: when 'comma fanboys' has already been used recently or too often, or when the comma has done enough work in other ways; and when the control unit introduced by it has enough impact to justify it.

We can profitably try the system out with another example. Here are nine sentences of varying length, just as you might scribble them down in drafting a rough paragraph. Study the possible connections between them:

1 **Science always improves.**
2 **Art never does.**
3 **The achievement of Newton has been superseded by Einstein.**

4 **The achievement of Euripides is in no way inferior to that of Shakespeare or Racine.**
5 **It is the purpose of science to learn in order to predict.**
6 **That helps us to select one of several quite crucial directions** between which we are usually trying to choose.
7 **It is in the nature of art to explore the already known,** in order that we may better understand the way we live.
8 **The advance of science is of unrivalled importance in our constant quest for improved lives.**
9 **The unchanging significance of art is that it is the means of evaluating the improvement and our response to life itself.**

The obvious feature here is the deliberate use of contrast by which the sentences proceed. The first control unit ('Science always improves') is immediately countered by the second ('Art never does'), thus forging a clear link between them; there is a case for 'comma fanboys' here, perhaps. The same is true of the contrast between the third and fourth sentences, and between the fifth and seventh; and the last two sentences are clearly an attempt to balance the same pair of thoughts that was introduced in the beginning. For this purpose of contrast, the classic 'fanboys' word is *but* (although *yet* is used for a stronger effect). Here is the revised paragraph:

> **Science constantly improves; art never does. The achievement of Newton has been susperseded by Einstein, but the achievement of Euripides is in no way inferior to that of Shakespeare or Racine. It is the purpose of science to learn in order to predict, for that helps us to select one of several quite crucial directions** between which we are usually trying to choose; **it is the nature of art to explore the already known,** in order that we may better understand the way we live. **The advance of science is of unrivalled importance in our constant quest for improved lives, but the unchanging significance of art is that it is the means of evaluating the improvement and our response to life itself.**

Nine sentences have been replaced by four, the stark viciousness of the full stops has disappeared in favour of an oiled smoothness, and the writer's intended meanings come out much more clearly.

So far, then, we have seen control units separated by the full stop, and linked and separated by the semicolon and 'comma fanboys'. Now it is time to deal briefly with the single dash and the colon, both of which have special uses covered in the next chapter.

The single dash can be followed by a word, a support unit, or (as here) a control unit:

> **The chairman's wife insisted on taking an interest in the business — she had seen too many 'office widows' end up in the divorce court.**

A full stop or a semicolon might have done the job instead of the dash. So might 'comma fanboys' — a comma followed by *for*. None of them would have had the extra touch of flair of the dash, which is a flamboyant mark. As we said before, this flamboyance is the dash's weakness as well as its strength, and you should use the mark sparingly. Too many dashes draw attention to themselves:

Wrong

> **Television, they say, is superior to radio — the combination of sight with sound is unbeatable. This is why some people are fonder of television than of radio — it is viewable as well as articulate. It is also one reason why television advertising costs so much — the commercials reach many more prospective buyers.**

That paragraph is suffering from a disease of dashes; it needs rescuing with the full stop, semicolon or 'comma fanboys'. Even more appropriate, perhaps, would be the colon, whose special use as an announcement mark suits any sentence in which the second part is a direct result or explanation of the first. All of the three sentences in the example fall into that category. So we can rewrite the example to much better effect, using 'comma fanboys', the colon, and a final, flaring dash:

> **Television, they say, is superior to radio, for the combination of sight with sound is unbeatable. This is why some people are fonder of television than of radio: it is viewable as well as articulate. It is also one reason why television advertising costs so much — the commercials reach many more prospective buyers.**

These, then, are the means open to you for linking clusters of meaning sensibly. There is a summary of them in Fig. 2.

*Fig. 2*  *Methods of separating or linking sentences*

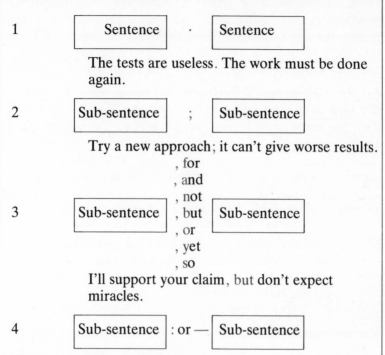

| 1 | Sentence | · | Sentence |

The tests are useless. The work must be done
again.

| 2 | Sub-sentence | ; | Sub-sentence |

Try a new approach; it can't give worse results.

| 3 | Sub-sentence | , for<br>, and<br>, not<br>, but<br>, or<br>, yet<br>, so | Sub-sentence |

I'll support your claim, but don't expect
miracles.

| 4 | Sub-sentence | : or — | Sub-sentence |

There's one thing he forgot: the machine he recommends
as the best just isn't available now.
The prison camp was full of officers — they had sworn to
die rather than be captured.

Notes:
(a) Sentences and sub-sentences consist of one control unit
each and perhaps an escort of support units.
(b) The full stop separates control units into full sentences.
The other systems yoke them together into the same
sentence, so a genuine link in meaning must be present
before these devices are used.
(c) The 'fanboys' words can be used after a semicolon if the
comma is at work already, or after a colon or dash when
the special effects of these marks are justified.

# Exercise 4

Here are two separate groups of sentences. Rewrite them, wavy-lining the control units and adding proper punctuation. (Note: middle stops have been deliberately omitted.) Then link the sentences in each group by choosing appropriate methods from those described in this chapter.

(a) The first proofs are usually sent out in galleys. These are long printed sheets not cut into page lengths. Two sets with the original typescript will be sent to the author. Of these two one set will generally be marked by the printer 'Marked Set' or 'Please return this set'. It contains the corrections marked by the printer to the errors he has not corrected in the type. It also contains queries raised by the printer. The author should make his corrections on the other set which he keeps. Then he should record them on the 'marked set' which he returns to the publisher. Great care should be taken when correcting proofs. Every error which is not the printer's adds to the cost of production. A single comma may cost 60 cents.

(b) With good discipline it is always possible to cram a student full of inert knowledge. You simply take a text book and make him learn it. The student then knows for instance how to calculate the square root of 1. What is the point of teaching him such a thing? The traditional answer to this views the mind as an instrument. You sharpen it first. Then you use it. Learning square roots is part of the sharpening process. This is the traditional answer. It is a dangerous concept. The mind is not a dead instrument. It is a living thing receptive to stimuli and hostile to a repressive harness. The purpose of education and it is one of the most difficult and frustrating challenges thrown in the face of men is to devise a harness so attractive that the pupil seeks it out voluntarily making the learning process enjoyable as well as profitable and self-disciplined.

# End Note

When 'comma fanboys' comes before a support unit (i.e., when the following sentence has a support unit placed first), the problem sometimes arises of whether or not to punctuate between them. The two sentences below will serve as a starting point:

1 **The minister responsible for the error should resign.**
2 Unless the Prime Minister sees him as a useful scapegoat, **the man's job is probably going to be safe.**

The appropriate 'fanboys' word is *but*. Logically, perhaps, the two sentences might be run together and puntuated thus:

**The minister responsible for the error should resign,** but, unless the Prime Minister sees him as a useful scapegoat, **the man's job is probably going to be safe.**

This is quite correct, but some readers will think there is one comma too many around 'but'. A useful way out is this:

**The minister responsible for the error should resign,** but unless the Prime Minister sees him as a useful scapegoat, **the man's job is probably going to be safe.**

This is a safe enough rule-of-thumb: when the support unit immediately after 'comma fanboys' is conditional (i.e., begins with words such as *if, unless, provided*), it is unnecessary to put a comma after the 'fanboys' word. Needless to say, always make sure that the omission of the comma will not cause the reader to misinterpret or get out of breath.

It is useful to close this chapter on the following note. The purpose of 'comma fanboys' and its associated middle stops is to link up sentences which might have been quite correct on their own. This linking should not really be done for its own sake, but whenever the needs of the paragraph demand it. The proper way of handling 'comma fanboys', therefore, is this: punctuate a sentence according to the needs of the *paragraph* rather than the needs of the sentence. The two earlier examples on the myth and on science and art should provide all the explanation needed, although the examples of paragraphs in the next chapter will serve as a further demonstration.

# 4 Essays and Paragraphs

The 'comma fanboys' system in Chapter 3 isn't just a cute method of describing how to join one sentence to another. It's also a way of preparing you for the business of writing paragraphs (look back at Exercise 4). Your techniques of writing paragraphs and essays could probably use a little dusting off, so what follows is a bundle of tricks of the trade that will surely increase your understanding and probably improve your performance.

All textbooks advocate essentially the same model of an essay. First, you make a plan of what you want to write. Second, you research the material implied by the plan. Third, you write an introduction which carefully embraces all the material, predicting the ways in which you are going to handle it. Then you develop the piece point by point, paragraph by paragraph. Finally, you write an ending that summarises your findings and perhaps draws conclusions. Many people do write in exactly this way, and it works well for them. As a model for the finished essay, in fact, it can hardly be bettered; its main achievement is to show that an essay, like any good Aristotelian, relies firmly on the sound structural principle of having a beginning, a middle, and an end.

Yet there are many writers who have difficulty writing to this prescription, which they take too literally. To them, making an early plan is really performing an act of clairvoyance, like predicting the winner of the 2.30 at Ascot. Any serious punter would probably give the little finger of his betting hand for the gift of foresight, a cruel sacrifice which is nevertheless what the standard essay model figuratively seems to demand. How can you know the result of a race until the race is over?

Fortunately, there is a human gift every bit as good as foresight, and all of us have it in lavish quantities. Its name is hindsight. The standard essay model, remember, is a model of the essay once it's finished; if it is the same model with which the writer starts out, well and good, but it doesn't have to be. When you examine a good essay, you will usually be able to derive an excellent plan from it. You will also think you can detect perfect foresight in the introductory paragraph. It may well be that way, but do not be deceived. One of the skills of writing an essay is to appear full of foresight, but there's a quite a good chance that the writer is really disguising a cunning act of hindsight. It depends which he finds easier. The difference between foresight and hindsight is the difference between deductive and inductive thinking: the deductive thinker applies known general truths to a series of particular observations, which is often the way an essay appears to work; the inductive thinker examines the particulars first and then draws conclusions from them, which is often what a writer actually does before he commits himself to his finished version. Every experienced writer knows that foresight is likely to be hindsight wearing a mask.

If all this is making you say, 'Yes, that's me!', this chapter is definitely for you. The following checklist might have looked a little weird before you read the last few paragraphs, but it ought to make a lot of sense to you now:

**Step 1:** Write the introduction last.
**Step 2:** Do your thinking before you write, not as you write.
**Step 3:** Write up each point separately.
**Step 4:** Find your control idea (the best connection between the points).
**Step 5:** Stitch the points together accordingly.
**Step 6:** Write the conclusion, then the introduction.

Let's take these one at a time.

## Six Steps for Essay Writing

*Step 1: Write the introduction last*

Like the opening scene in a film or a play, the first paragraph of an essay has a powerful function. It introduces the main idea and suggests ways in which the writer might develop them. Obviously, there can be a gap between intention and achievement; other ideas may occur during the writing which you will be tempted to follow up. That is why an essay will be the better for being revised, but it is also why the introduction will be the better for being left till last. This becomes truer as the writing becomes lengthier. Any textbook writer is likely to tell you that the preface to a book is not usually written until the book itself is finished; you can't introduce something which doesn't yet exist.

The easiest way of writing a good introduction is to describe the reason for the essay's existence — the central idea or purpose. Different books have different names for this central idea: the most common are 'proposition', 'theme', 'topic', and 'thesis'. As you have presumably read the earlier chapters, it might reinforce this book's interest in the principle of structure if we call this thesis the control idea — in kinship with the control unit explained in Chapter 2. The **control idea** controls everything you write in the essay; it dictates how each paragraph is handled, each argument shaped. And the supporting ideas and arguments, the supporting sentences, are exactly that: **supports** — in kinship with the support unit, which is also explained in Chapter 2. The structural principle is exactly the same. Just as a sentence needs a control unit, so an essay needs a control idea. And, unless you're lucky or skilful enough to hit on that idea immediately, and then to stick to it throughout your first draft, you must wait for it to arise from your notes. It is certainly useful to have a control idea right at the start, but don't treat it as sacred. Think of it simply as a working hypothesis, and allow it to change, if necessary, as your ideas mature. It doesn't matter when you find your control idea; it only matters that you do find it. Sticking grimly to an original version of a control idea is a technique that's forced on you under examination conditions. There is absolutely no need to hamstring yourself by using examination techniques when you have a week or more to write your essay.

*Step 2: Do your thinking before you write, not as you write*

This is really a re-statement of the above. If you have forty-five minutes to write an answer, you have precious little time to think at length and none at all to take notes. If you have a two-thousand-word essay on your hands, and a corresponding amount of time, not only is it unnecessary to get it right first time, but the odds against doing so are huge. As the essay lengthens, so do the odds.

So don't write formally until you've done your thinking and note-taking. At this early stage, do whatever is most comfortable. Scratch early thoughts down on the back of an envelope, a message pad, an exercise book, a clean sheet of paper, an index card — anything at all that you can cope with and keep organised. Do the same with quotations you may want to use. Hint: for a long essay, keep each thought, note, and quote separate. That way they're easier to use. If you keep notes on the same sheet of paper, you can easily become lost in the morass of words. Use different sheets, cards, etc., for different notes. Paper is cheap; time isn't.

## Step 3: Write up each point separately

Your early scratchings will generate a number of points you'll want to discuss more thoroughly. Take a fresh sheet of paper for each point (this is where the advice of the last paragraph begins to pay off). Head it with a brief statement of the topic; one word will do, but don't be afraid to use a phrase or a sentence. Then start writing. If you can organise as you go, so that your thoughts fall out of your mind in a ready-made logical order, fine. If not, don't worry. Just go on till you've exhausted everything you want to say. You might produce a short paragraph, or three or four longer ones, but keep going till you finish. (If you run out of steam, put the sheet aside for a while and go on to the next.) When you finish, put that sheet aside and start the same process for the next point. And so on. When you've completed all your separate discussions, you'll have a series of miniature essays to form the basis of your text. You might even find that you have your essay in front of you, without serious revision.

Now concentrate on each of those sheets in turn. They may look like a garbled mess, but never fear. Your achievement so far is a big one: you have split the work into convenient, bite-sized chunks, which concentrates the mind wonderfully. Go through each point, revising this sentence, removing that, adding another, re-locating a fourth. Organise the paragraph(s). Aim early to find a key sentence for each paragraph, one that seems to 'lead' the others. If you can't find one, write one. What you're looking for, to use this book's terminology again, is a **control sentence** — a sentence which all other sentences support. (Alternative terms are 'topic sentence', 'thesis sentence', 'proposition sentence', and so on. The basic structural principle is important; what you call it isn't.) The essay needs a control idea, the paragraph a control sentence, and the sentence a control unit. You'll find examples and further discussion under **Beginnings, Middles, Ends** and under **Paragraph Types** (coming shortly).

*Step 4: Find your control idea (the best connection between the points)*

Each paragraph now has a control sentence. Look at all the control sentences together. What you're looking for is a common factor, a shared target, a connection between them which you can describe, preferably in a single sentence. All paragraphs should be working towards this one end, which must be important enough to justify your whole essay. This is your **control idea**, your reason for writing the finished essay. Apart from being a device which organises all paragraphs written so far, it is important enough to play a significant part in the conclusion and the introduction. You may have had this control idea right from the start, or it might have been rising gradually to the surface of your mind throughout the three earlier steps. If not, the surprise you get when you do finally see it will be that much nicer.

All paragraphs should support the control idea. If you have a control which most of your paragraphs fit, stay with it even if a couple of paragraphs look a little uncomfortable. Try to re-shape the unhappy paragraphs to fit, but if you can't — jettison them. Always be prepared to discard. Equally, always be ready to write something new to tie in with your new-found control idea. You may be short of your quota of words, or you may have recently thought of another discussion point. Such a point will often occur to you when an identifiable control idea begins to take command of its material. Stay flexible.

The main benefit to the writer of working out a control idea is organisational. It immediately influences the relative importance of the individual items the essay deals with, and determines the amount of space spent on them and the order in which they are tackled. It provides a framework in which raw material can find its proper place. It offers a touchstone, a sort of court of appeal by whose standards the importance of the material can be judged, and its constant presence keeps the essay relevant. The two recurrent questions, 'How do I use this?' and 'Do I really need that at all?', are much more easily answered when the essay has a control idea that is never very far away.

You now have your essay, rough though it may still be. It's time to sculpt the edges and smooth the rough bits.

## *Step 5: Stitch the points together accordingly*

Your paragraphs might well dictate their own order in the procession. That's a hallmark of a good essay. But you might find that the procession is still a little disjointed. One paragraph may fit well with its predecessor, but awkwardly with the one that follows. Re-write the opening or closing of one of them to make them sit snugly together. You must see that the paragraphs flow smoothly along, developing the argument rather than kangaroo-hopping. See under **Paragraph Hooks** later.

In **Step 4** you make the paragraphs fit a control idea, like struts under an umbrella. In **Step 5** you make them fit together, like links in a chain.

## *Step 6: Write the conclusion, then the introduction*

These will nearly write themselves by now, but perhaps not quite. Spend some time getting them right. A good conclusion rounds off the essay with a satisfying sense of inevitability; a good introduction presents the reader with just the right information in just the right way to help him to read intelligently. Your stitched paragraphs should lead you remorselessly to a summarising point of closure and, even more readily, to that introductory level of hindsight which looks so much like foresight. One difference between introduction and conclusion is that the former is a preliminary survey of the territory, perhaps looking forward to obvious landmarks or cautioning against hidden dangers. 'That path is a safe one,' one introduction might say. 'Here be dragons,' another may warn. Either way, the reader is being briefed by a guide who has already covered the territory. The conclusion, on the other hand, is a brief report of the guided tour; it is more *experienced* than the introduction. To invoke Aristotle, a beginning is that which nothing can precede but from which something must follow, while a conclusion is that which something must precede but which nothing can follow.

It is difficult to discuss openings and closings without examples. These follow under '**Beginnings, Middles, Ends**'.

## Paragraph Types

Broadly speaking, there are two types of paragraph: one illustrates a point, the other develops it. It is possible to sub-classify these types, or to make different classifications altogether, but illustration and development will serve as simple and effective categories. The **illustrative** paragraph explains a point you have already established, in that paragraph or an earlier one, and it frequently becomes a kind of gigantic parenthesis; its advantage is that it clarifies, but it leaves you vulnerable to the danger of interrupting the essay. The **developmental** paragraph, on the other hand, moves the argument along and creates a firm sense of going somewhere.

### The Illustrative Paragraph

Think of a paragraph as if it were a huge sentence. Think of that sentence as being constructed with a colon: a main point is made first, and an explanation follows immediately. Take this sentence: 'Different cultures have different words for the same thing: South African, Australian, and American English draw from different vocabularies to describe the English farm or the English tramp.' Now see how that colon-construction is structurally similar to the following illustrative paragraph:

**The words that constitute the hoard of the English language differ from country to country**. In England, the motor of a car is under a *bonnet*, not a *hood*, and its occupants are protected by a *windscreen*, not a *windshield*. An Englishman will do *straight away* what an American will do *right away*. One rides on the *Underground* in London, not the *subway* as in America; and an Australian drives under a *subway* where an Englishman drives under a *railway bridge*. What is a *ranch* to an American is a *farm* to an Englishman and a *station* to an Australian. The English *tramp* or the American *hobo* turns into a *swaggie* or *swagman* when he goes down under. In South Africa a village is a *dorp*, a foreman a *baas*, a hill is a *kopje*, a movie a *bioscope*, a wagon trip a *trek*, and a porch a *stoep*. We see, then, that the vocabulary of English is not uniform, but is different wherever we go.

If this were a sentence, there would be a colon after the second 'country'. The paragraph is too long and complex to be a single sentence, but the structure is the same; the **support sentences** deliver the goods promised by the **control sentence**, placed first. The structure allows the paragraph to gather momentum. It starts by establishing the control sentence, then branches out into full **support sentences**, and then, its base secure, spreads a net of support units in the penultimate sentence to carry the load until the control can be re-asserted at the end. It is a fairly well-paced paragraph of the illustrative kind, and there are many occasions when this kind of paragraph is useful. But the example shows the weakness of its kind as well as the strength: the more it tells you, the more it slows you down. An example, by definition, does not readily permit forward progress. It is an interruption.

## The Developmental Paragraph

The paragraph that develops an idea has much more thrust than one that illustrates an idea. It states that idea in the control sentence, and uses its supports to take the idea further. This kind of paragraph pushes forward all the time, and for that reason is intellectually meatier. The following example from George Steiner* will make the point.

---

* George Steiner, 'Humane Literacy', in *Language and Silence* (Harmondsworth: Pelican, 1969), p. 23.

At the end of his previous paragraph, Steiner asserted that 'some of the men who devised and administered Auschwitz had been trained to read Shakespeare or Goethe'. He sees great significance in this, and opens a new paragraph to question the traditional claim of the humanities subjects that learning to appreciate the arts is a civilising process which makes people's real-life behaviour more humane:

> **This is of obvious and appalling relevance to the study and teaching of literature**. It compels us to ask whether knowledge of the best that has been thought and said does, as Matthew Arnold asserted, broaden and refine the resources of the human spirit. It forces us to wonder whether what Dr Leavis has called 'the central humanity' [literature] does, in fact, educate towards humane action, or whether there is not between the tenor of the moral intelligence developed in the study of literature and that required in social and political choice, a wide gap or contrariety. The latter possibility is particularly disturbing. There is some evidence that a trained, persistent commitment to the life of the printed word, a capacity to identify deeply and critically with imaginary personages or sentiments, diminishes the immediacy, the hard edge of actual circumstance. We come to respond more acutely to the literary sorrow than to the misery next door. Here also recent times give hard evidence. Men who wept at Werther or Chopin moved, unrealising, through literal hell.

Steiner states his control first, then examines why he finds the case of Auschwitz appallingly relevant to the arts. In his support sentences he suggests that the humanities may not humanise (the 'wide gap' between aim and achievement), and even puts forward the example of the Auschwitz officers and administrators (those 'who wept at Werther or Chopin') as evidence of a 'contrariety', of the frightening possibility that the supposedly humanising arts might actually de-humanise — that people who respond deeply to art may somehow diminish their ability to respond to life. The paragraph moves forward all the time, broaching new ideas when it has to, but never forgetting to subordinate them to the meaning of 'appalling relevance' in the control sentence.

You can use both the illustrative and the developmental paragraphs, and you can use a combination of both (even developmental paragraphs often contain examples). In general, however, give preference to the developmental. It is vital to maintain an essay's forward motion with a minimum of interruptions.

## Beginnings, Middles, Ends

Writing the beginning and the end of an essay involves a sense of strategy; the entire essay is hinted at and commented on through the control idea. Writing the middle paragraphs (that is, all except the first and the last) involves a sense of tactics; every paragraph should be firmly coupled to the ones before and after, and should additionally support the control idea expressed in the opening.

The following sample paragraphs are taken from an essay written by a student, Ed Lacy, in a course which includes film criticism. The film he is writing about is Francis Ford Coppola's *Apocalypse Now*. His control idea is that the traditional myth of the American hero as the defender of virtue, freedom, and moral values (such as you will find in many older Westerns and war films) must be turned on its head: that this particular film enacts a critique of American society, its motivations and beliefs. His notes included many points which he later turned into an eleven-paragraph, two-thousand-word essay. Four of those paragraphs will be quoted here.

Ed's introduction is a brief statement of relevant background (the important word is 'relevant'), which he almost immediately hitches to the subject of film, ending with a short statement of his control idea:

Opening paragraph

Nothing has been more injurious to the American dream than defeat in Vietnam. It was much more than a military setback; it was an ideological humiliation. America, the father of democracy and guardian of human freedom, had been worsted by an ill-equipped and under-nourished foe who also happened to be communist. It was a defeat which conflicted directly with the mythology of America's wild west, from which had emerged the archetypal hero of a thousand Hollywood films: broad of shoulder and narrow of hip, he rode interminably across the open plain, a symbol of truth and freedom. In combat his courage and powers of leadership were as much taken for granted as the code of honour which governed his every action. Francis Ford Coppola's *Apocalypse Now*, on the other hand, uses the wild west myths as contrasts between the frontiersman of American folklore and the serviceman in Vietnam. **The contrast is one of inversion: traditional concepts of the hero and the open range, the efficiency of command, the nature of courage and discipline, and America's role as the self-appointed agent of freedom and democracy, are shown to be totally out of accord with the new realities of Vietnam.**

There are several things to notice. First, it is a big paragraph; there are seven sentences of comfortably varying length and construction, which give the writer plenty of time to say what he needs to. Second, the historical background is not just empty, half-relevant waffle designed merely to get the writer's juices flowing; it bears directly on the control idea. Third, there is an easy glide from that background into its manifestations in film. Fourth, the same comfortable glide leads from film generally to the one film the writer intends to discuss. Fifth, the paragraph is designed to spear in to a sharp statement of what the essay is going to do: this is the control idea expressed by the last sentence. Sixth, that control sentence hints economically at the essay's topic: that it will deal with concepts of the hero, etc., and that the concepts will be seen through a series of contrasts. Ed Lacy has encapsulated his whole essay, the strategy as well as the topic, in the one paragraph. It is an excellent beginning.

That is the way of beginnings. You make statements of general relevance which narrow to a sharp statement of the control idea. The opening paragraph is the only one where you should aim almost invariably to have the control sentence at the end. Other paragraphs state their control sentences wherever they wish (although it is usual to start with them), but the opening paragraph is almost always best when the control sentence (and hence the control idea) is stated last.

By the time he has finished typing his essay, Ed has covered all the points he anticipated in his introduction. (Obviously. He wrote the introduction knowing what to anticipate. Hindsight, remember?) He then had the option of summarising each point in his concluding paragraph, but he chose instead to reinforce the points from a slightly different angle. *Apocalypse Now* contains a minor metaphor, the word 'home', which stands lightly in the film for all the qualities of democracy, freedom, virtue and heroism which the film questions. This is how he handles his concluding paragraph:

Final Paragraph

The modern frontiersman, then, finds his progress halted by the jungle, a symbol of the impenetrable and mysterious system of values against which, thoroughly bewildered, he must now set himself. *Apocalypse Now* shows the erosion in modern America of the humanistic system of values which had its origins in the myth of the wild west. At the beginning of the film, Willard is depressed and disoriented because, like the other servicemen, he is unable to convince himself that he is fighting for anything worthwhile — even that there is anything worth fighting for at all. In his Saigon hotel room, he says: 'When I was here, I wanted to go home. When I was home, I wanted to be back here.' He no longer recognises what home is, especially as its so-called virtues are represented in the film by the frightening figure of Colonel Kilgore, the officer who destroys a village so that his men can go surfing. At nightfall in a jungle clearing, Willard watches with quiet irony as Kilgore attempts to re-create, with campfire and guitar, the feel of the open range. 'The harder he tried to make it feel like home,' says Willard, 'the further away it seemed. Home didn't exist any more.' **In Kilgore, as in *Apocalypse Now* as a whole, the status of America as the supporter of freedom and democracy is shown to be badly flawed indeed.**

Because of the full treatment of the discussion points in the nine middle paragraphs of the essay, the conclusion can touch on them with an economy that enables the writer to embrace the spirit of the film simply by allowing that single metaphor, 'home', to summarise all he wishes to say. Notice also that positive feeling of finality in the last sentence. Aristotle's lesson that nothing can follow an ending has been well learned.

So much for beginnings and ends. Ed Lacy's middle paragraphs are similarly well put together. Here are two examples. In the first, the control sentence comes a third of the way through (control sentences can occur anywhere — first, last, or in between):

47

## Middle Paragraph

America's intervention in Vietnam was chiefly motivated by ideological fervour, by a powerful belief in her role as the ambassador of freedom and democracy. Servicemen reinforced these notions of national superiority by referring contemptuously to the Vietcong and North Vietnamese as 'gooks' or 'Charlie', thereby de-personalising the enemy and vindicating, in advance, any atrocities perpetrated against him. ***Apocalypse Now* inverts these notions in a series of images which contrast the inhumanity of American servicemen with the vulnerability of a North Vietnamese village.** As Colonel Kilgore's helicopter assault (the modern version of a cavalry charge) thunders towards this village, the viewer is struck by the scene of peace and serenity below: tall, green breakers roll majestically shorewards; peasants labour industriously in the paddy fields; and a schoolmistress in a blouse of pure white supervises her class on a wide courtyard of well-scrubbed stone. These images connote peace, simplicity, innocence, and purity; and the helicopter attack comes as a gross intrusion on the idyllic scene. This is not simply a surprise attack on the enemy; the village is being symbolically raped. This intuition is supported when the schoolmistress is violated by machine-gun bullets, her pure white blouse becoming instantaneously a torn and bloodied rag. With her dies the notion of America as the representative of justice and freedom. Kilgore and his men bring sorrow where there was joy, and death where there was life. His justification? One of his men is a surfing champion, and the coastline by the village offers the best surf in Vietnam.

Note how all sentences support the control sentence. To put it the other way, note how the control sentence *does* control: it encapsulates the entire paragraph. The paragraph has somewhere to go, and the control sentence is leading it there. See also that the control sentence bears directly on the control idea, the last sentence in the opening paragraph. Finally, see how the last sentence in this paragraph carries that note of finality: that quiet statement is all that is needed to put a shattering perspective on two hundred and fifty words.

That middle paragraph is unmistakably developmental, but it uses examples to help it develop. The same is true of the next sample, a paragraph which comes immediately after the one just quoted (note the words 'but' and 'also' which act as links between the two):

**But Kilgore's attack also provides a powerful contrast between the absolute personal commitment of the North Vietnamese and the lack of real determination amongst the Americans.** As the helicopters approach, the former move quickly, but with a sense of order and control, to makeshift defensive positions. The villagers are hopelessly vulnerable, but their sense of purpose never falters. Colonel Kilgore, on the other hand, calls the attack off when one of his helicopters, injudicious enough to land in the village, is destroyed by a hand grenade. ('F . . . ing savages,' mutters Kilgore.) For Kilgore, the attack is a 'piece of action' for his boys, and he will commit them only to the extent that no large sacrifices are made. His attitude is symptomatic of America's failure in the war. For the enemy, war meant total commitment. They acknowledged only two possibilities: death or victory.

This time the control sentence is the first. An example is used, but is strictly controlled by need: 'the helicopters approach', it begins, but only to show the villagers' 'sense of order and control' and their 'sense of purpose'. This is used to contrast with the American attitude that this piece of savagery is merely a 'piece of action', which is only worthwhile provided 'no large sacrifices are made'. This is a developmental paragraph which nevertheless makes use of an example. See how the control sentence provides a model for this approach: Kilgore's attack (the example) provides a powerful contrast between the Americans and the North Vietnamese (the purpose). Like the preceding paragraph, furthermore, this one is hitched directly to the control idea in the opening paragraph. That's important. Look and see.

# Paragraph Hooks

Every paragraph should flow from the one before. This should come naturally in a developmental essay, but it is possible that your first draft may bump and jar between paragraphs. This is especially likely once you have completed your write-ups of paragraph points (see **Steps 3** and **5** earlier), as each of these might be written before the big control idea is fully formed, and therefore before you know for certain how the paragraphs are going to fit together. The best way of fitting them together is by 'hooking' them — writing in a bridging word or phrase, or making sure that the idea discussed in one paragraph is resumed in the next, even if from a different point of view. In the second of Ed Lacy's middle paragraphs quoted earlier, the writer used the simple 'but' and 'also' in his first sentence to hook the paragraph firmly into its predecessor ('*But* Kilgore's attack *also* provides a powerful contrast . . .'). If you remove those words, you'll see what the paragraph may have looked like in **Steps 3** and **4**; put them back in, and you'll see how easy it is to hook two similar paragraphs together. For a more complex example, let's use the end and the beginning of two adjacent paragraphs from George Steiner, quoted earlier in this chapter. Suppose Steiner had written them like this:

No Hook

. . . We know that some of the men who devised and administered Auschwitz had been trained to read Shakespeare or Goethe, and continued to do so.

We are compelled to ask whether knowledge of the best that has been thought and said does, as Matthew Arnold asserted, broaden and refine the resources of the human spirit. . . .

The opening of the second paragraph is too much of a break; there is no strong connection with the end of the first. This is how Steiner actually wrote it:

Hook

. . . We know that some of the men who devised and administered Auschwitz had been trained to read Shakespeare or Goethe, and continued to do so.

This is of obvious and appalling relevance to the study or teaching of literature. It compels us to ask whether knowledge of the best that has been thought and said does, as Matthew Arnold asserted, broaden and refine the resources of the human spirit. . . .

The addition of that opening sentence does two things. It hooks into the preceding paragraph with the simple word 'this', and it also provides a control sentence which gives the new paragraph the leadership it may have lacked otherwise. The original version might have done, if only barely; Steiner's actual version is much better.

There are different kinds of hook. Signpost words or phrases (see Chapter 5) are the simplest and the most

50

common: 'this', 'that', 'admittedly', 'however', 'in spite of that', 'it is nevertheless true', 'furthermore', 'less surprisingly', 'on the other hand', 'to begin with', and so on. The list of options is almost infinite. A second kind of hook involves some repetition:

## Repeat Hook

. . . He appeared to be almost universally regarded as a lightweight, superficial, ageing movie star.
     The ageing movie star was to go on to win the next Presidential election with a big majority. . . .

The effect of this device is quite strong, and its obvious stylistic impact is the very reason why its use should be restricted. Over-exposure will make it look a little arch, coy, self-conscious. The third main kind of hook can be used much more often, because it is as discreet as it is effective. This hook embeds itself in an idea rather than a word or phrase. For example: 'It is precisely the fear of alienating their audiences that caused the earlier Hollywood films to steer clear of anything resembling bad taste'; 'Such a view is commonly held only by politicians of the more conservative type'; or 'It is much harder to take sides with conviction when further facts are revealed'. Here is a longer example, taken from an article by Stuart Hood:

## Idea hook

. . . a high official in the trade union movement has been heard to express the view that because the BBC is independent it might not be proper to exert . . . pressures. What the TUC and individual unions have yet to learn is how to apply them at both national and local levels.
     The occasions when the broadcasting organisations acknowledge pressure from bodies of opinion outside the conventional spectrum are rare. . . .*

The idea hook ( and the word) is 'pressure', but it is the rest of the sentence that shows the connection fully and also suggests how the new paragraph is going to develop.
     You will see by now that your own use of the paragraph hook is quite frequent, if perhaps unconscious, and will often present no problem in an essay which flows naturally

---

* Stuart Hood, 'The Politics of Television', in Denis McQuail (ed.), *Sociology of Mass Communication* (Harmondsworth: Penguin, 1976), p. 421.

to begin with. But it is after **Steps 3** and **5** that a conscious awareness of the device will become beneficial.

# Exercise 5

The first paragraph is taken (with the addition of one word) from Stanley Milgram's 'A Behavioural Study of Obedience' in *The Journal of Abnormal and Social Psychology*, 1963. The second is a paragraph based on the same article. The third is the opening paragraph of Jacob Bronowski's essay 'The Creative Mind in Science and Art' in his *Science and Human Values* (New York: Harper and Row, 1965). In (a) and (b), find the control sentence for each paragraph. Are these paragraphs illustrative, developmental, or a mixture of both? In (c), devise a better control sentence that fits at the end of the paragraph and encapsulates its essence.

(a) Obedience is as basic an element in the structure of social life as one can point to. Some system of authority is a requirement of all communal living, and it is only the man dwelling in isolation who is not forced to respond, through defiance or submission, to the commands of others. Furthermore, obedience as a determinant of behaviour is of particular relevance to our time. It has been reliably established that from 1933–1945 millions of innocent persons were systematically slaughtered on command. Gas chambers were built, death camps were guarded, daily quotas of corpses were produced with the same efficiency as the manufacture of appliances. These inhumane policies may have originated in the mind of a single person, but they could only be carried out on a massive scale if a very large number of persons obeyed orders.

(b) An experiment was set up whereby randomly selected persons were invited to take part in what was called a 'learning process'. They were asked to deliver electric shocks of increasing voltages to a volunteer victim, no matter how much pain was inflicted. They did not know that the electric generator was a dummy and that the 'victim' was acting a part; they believed the electricity was real and the victim was in great suffering. The amazing result was that every single person not only continued to give what he thought were agonising shocks, but did so without coercion other than obedience to the reminder that he was taking part in a scientific experiment. The often-repeated experiment suggests the horrifying finding that ordinary people will inflict great pain on others through simple obedience. There were some extenuating circumstances — the experiment took place at reputable Yale University, the supervisor looked impressively scientific, and the victim was known to be a volunteer — but there was nothing that really diminishes the bare fact of the result.

(c) No scientific theory is a collection of facts. It will not even do to call a theory true or false in the simple sense in which every fact is either so or not so. The Epicureans held that matter is made of atoms two thousand years ago, and we are now tempted to say that their theory was true. But if we do so, we confuse their notion of matter with our own. John Dalton in 1808 first saw the structure of matter as we do today, and what he took from the ancients was not their theory but something richer, their image: the atom. Much of what was in Dalton's mind was as vague as the Greek notion, and quite as mistaken. But he suddenly gave life to the new facts of chemistry and the ancient theory together, by fusing them to give what neither had: a coherent picture of how matter is linked and built up from different kinds of atoms. The act of fusion is the creative act.

# 5 Middle Stops

Middle stops are those which appear before the end of a sentence and which signal the existence of a word, or words, to be regarded as distinct from others in the sentence. They are the comma, the semicolon, the colon, the dash, and brackets; they do not include the full stop, the exclamation mark and the question mark, which terminate a sentence and are therefore end stops. See Chapters 1, 2 and 3 in conjunction with the following pages.

## The Comma (,)

The comma is a grammatical separator. It represents a pause in meaning, not a pause for breath. It is the lightest of all the stops, and the most abused. Its correct use is vital, for this casual little mark can affect the entire meaning of the words around it.

### *The Comma with* and

The simplest use of the comma is in separating a series of items. Sometimes a comma before *and* is crucial:

> Many of the plays of that time were written by Shakespeare, Marlowe, Kyd, Webster, Beaumont and Fletcher and Ford.

Because there are no commas before the last two *ands*, you have a pretty good idea that some of the plays referred to were written by more than one author. But did Beaumont collaborate with Fletcher? Did Fletcher collaborate with Ford? Or did all three collaborate with each other? The problem arises because the writer here was trying to apply the mistaken rule that you never put a comma before *and*. The problem disappears with an appropriately placed comma:

> Many of the plays of that time were written by Shakespeare, Marlowe, Kyd, Webster, Beaumont and Fletcher, and Ford.

That final comma separates the last name from the others, and we see that Beaumont and Fletcher are the collaborators. Such is the value of a well-placed comma.

### *The Comma with* which *and* who

Once again, your decision to use or omit a comma depends entirely on common sense. Suppose you wanted to say that the kind of government you most respect is not only the elected kind but the kind which always tells the truth. You would be wrong to write this:

Wrong
> **An elected government**, which always tells the truth, **is the one I most respect.** *

As it stands, you are saying that every elected government always tells the truth. Sad to say, this is not necessarily so, and it is certainly not what you meant. The gist of that sentence is that you respect every elected government, and that you do so *because* they all tell the truth. And that isn't what you meant, either. That pair of commas creates a middle support unit introduced by *which*, but there shouldn't be a middle support unit at all: 'An elected government which always tells the truth' is the subject group, and the sentence is one complete control unit (see Chapter 2). This is what you meant to say:

> **An elected government which always tells the truth is the one I most respect.**

Here's an easy guide: test to see if you can use 'that' instead of 'which'. If you can, don't put a comma before it. If you can't, use 'which' with a comma. This test will show you the meaning of the sentence, and a good punctuator punctuates according to meaning. He knows that a strict grammatical rule of the narrow-minded variety can

---

* As before, bold type identifies control units; light, support units.

sometimes get him into trouble. Suppose we created out of thin air a law that says we must always put a comma before *who*. If so, then one of these two sentences would have to be wrong:

> Members of Alcoholics Anonymous helped the drunk who fell off the bus.
> Members of Alcoholics Anonymous helped the drunk, who fell off the bus.

The only difference is the comma. But what a difference! In the first sentence, 'who fell off the bus' is not separated from 'the drunk' and is therefore part of the same word group — in short, it does the job of a single adjective and tells us that the drunk we are hearing about is that particular drunk who fell off the bus. The whole sentence is a control unit, which (remember?) can't usually be broken up by a single middle stop. In the second sentence, therefore, that comma must mean that 'who fell off the bus' is not a part of the control unit but a free-standing, fully fledged support unit. If we again use bold type to identify the control unit, the bizarre meaning of this sentence should be clear:

> **Members of Alcoholics Anonymous helped the drunk**, who fell off the bus.

The comma — seemingly innocent but so often deadly — has turned a statement into a warning: if you ever get drunk on a bus, don't let Alcoholics Anonymous get anywhere near you. You might fall off.

## *The Comma with Signposts*

There's an impressive stockpile to choose from when you want to signpost the twists and turns in your thinking. These signposts begin with the seven 'fanboys' words you came across in Chapter 3 — *for, and, nor, but, or, yet*, and *so*. They interrupt the flow of the sentence in order to change its direction. One such word is *however:*

> His temper is too uncontrollable for him to be a really good politician. However, he's the likeliest candidate we've got.

> I agree that you have always contributed well to class discussions, Michelle. Your performance as an essayist, however, leaves a lot to be desired.

Signpost words bring the sequence of thought skidding round in a U-turn and send your reader off along the path you want him to follow. Unlike the seven 'fanboys' words, they very frequently appear in the middle of the control unit, and they almost always demand punctuation on both sides. See Fig. 3 for a fuller description.

*Fig. 3   Some signpost words*

| | |
|---|---|
| Addition | again, also, and then, besides, equally, finally, first, first of all, furthermore, in addition, in fact, in the first place, in the next place, last, likewise, moreover, next, second, too, what is more. |
| | Approximate 'fanboys' equivalents: *and, or* (not followed by a comma). |
| Cause/effect/ reason | accordingly, as a result, becaue of this, consequently, hence, in short, for this reason, otherwise, then, therefore, thus. |
| | Approximate 'fanboys' equivalents: *for, so* (not followed by a comma). |
| Comparison | also, in the same way, likewise, similarly. |
| | Approximate 'fanboys' equivalent: *or* (not followed by a comma). |
| Concession | admittedly, after all, although true, at the same time, even though . . ., naturally, obviously, of course. |
| | Approximate 'fanboys' equivalents: *but, yet* (not followed by a comma). |
| Contrast | after all, although true, and yet, at the same time, for all that, however, in contrast, in spite of . . ., nevertheless, nonetheless, notwithstanding, on the contrary, on the other hand, still. |
| | Approximate 'fanboys' equivalents: *but, or, nor, yet* (not followed by a comma). |

The essence of signpost words (again with the exception of 'fanboys') is that they are deliberately interruptive; your reader must always know about it whenever you push one at him. This explains the need for punctuation which separates the signpost word from all the others without breaking everything into fragments — in short, it explains the need for a comma. Put a comma after a signpost if it is the first word or phrase in the sentence;* put a comma before it if it is the last word in the sentence;* and surround it with a comma pair if it comes elsewhere within the sentence.

This is not a complete list, and the categories sometimes overlap. Apart from the 'fanboys' words (see Chapter 3), most of these signposts often pop up *inside* the control unit. Treat them as support units and punctuate with commas accordingly; this will prevent misreading.

## The Comma versus the Full Stop

One of the most frequent and irritating writing faults is known as the comma splice — the illogical use of the comma instead of the full stop or its equivalent (see Chapter 3).

Wrong

The German defeat was already a military fact before Berlin was taken, Allied strategists considered that the occupation of the capital was psychologically vital.

Two control units have been scrambled together in the kind of shotgun marriage which characterises much poor writing. That comma should have been followed by *but*, or removed entirely and replaced with a full stop or a semicolon. The point has been made before, but it is made again here because surgery on the comma splice sometimes meets complications — in particular the belief that adding a signpost word somehow justifies a comma. It's a nice try, but it's wrong:

---

* That is, if the signpost comes directly after a full stop, semicolon, colon or dash. If it comes directly before or after 'comma fanboys', you may want to convert to 'semicolon fanboys' to avoid a plague of commas. See Fig. 2 and the attached explanation.

**Wrong**

The German defeat was already a military fact before Berlin was taken, *however* Allied strategists considered that the occupation of the capital was psychologically vital.

**Wrong**

The German defeat was already a military fact before Berlin was taken, *however,* Allied strategists considered that the occupation of the capital was psychologically vital.

It doesn't matter whether you use a comma or a comma pair — the separation of the control units is still too weak. The only signpost words which can get away with a comma alone when joining control units are the 'fanboys' words; all the others need a stronger stop, usually the semicolon or an end stop. This is the way to do it:

The German defeat was already a military fact before Berlin was taken; *however,* Allied strategists considered that the occupation of the capital was psychologically vital.

The felony is compounded here (specifically in the second wrong example) by a quirk of meaning. Like many English words, *however* has more than one use. As a signpost word, it has roughly the meaning of *but*, as we have seen; in that usage it must invariably take a comma. But it can also mean *no matter how*, and is then an incomplete statement which requires an instant follow-up with no separating punctuation:

**I can't understand this pesky business about comma splices,** *however* hard I try.

As usual, the bold type identifies the control unit, and it is easy to see that *however* is here being used as the first word of a support unit and not as a signpost. In this usage, the word invariably does *not* take a comma after it. The difference in the two meanings of this word ought to underline the reason why signpost words usually clamour for a comma; they are support units, whether they consist of one word or several, and support units have the right to protect themselves with punctuation against the main thrust of the sentence.

# Exercise 6

Write out the following pairs of sentences, explaining the different meanings of each and identifying control units with a wavy underline.

1 (a) Only students with anti-litter banners can patrol the streets with large dogs.
  (b) Only students, with anti-litter banners, can patrol the streets with large dogs.
2 (a) This is the tutorial room where we have some of our best classes.
  (b) This is the tutorial room, where we have some of our best classes.
3 (a) He was not cheerful because he fell in the water.
  (b) He was not cheerful, because he fell in the water.
4 (a) The truth I discovered was more painful to him than anything else.
  (b) The truth, I discovered, was more painful to him than anything else.
5 (a) The best policeman is the Irishman who is large enough and vocal enough to inspire respect.
  (b) The best policeman is the Irishman, who is large enough and vocal enough to inspire respect.
6 (a) He was immediately set upon by the dwarf who beat him to within an inch of his life.
  (b) He was immediately set upon by the dwarf, who beat him to within an inch of his life.
7 (a) The cure for hydrophobia long eluded discovery, however the French scientist Louis Pasteur sought for it.
  (b) The cure for hydrophobia long eluded discovery; however, the French scientist, Louis Pasteur, sought for it.
8 (a) The actress sued her next-door neighbour, an archbishop and a truly moral man.
  (b) The actress sued her next-door neighbour, an archbishop, and a truly moral man.
9 (a) I shall treat it as a simple matter of course.
  (b) I shall treat it as a simple matter, of course.
10 (a) When I last heard of him he was still acting naturally.

(b) When I last heard of him he was still acting, naturally.

# The Semicolon (;)

This stop is a kind of traveller's rest on the way from the comma to the full stop. It has the qualities of both, but is stronger than the first and weaker than the second, so its uses are limited. The two main duties of the semicolon are described below; see also Chapter 3.

## The Semicolon as a List Separator

The semicolon can sometimes do the job of a comma, but only when the comma is already at work on a lighter task. This usually happens when you list items in a series, because some of the items have to be split up into sub-items. Here are two sentences which use the comma to separate items:

> He was famous for his wit, his charm, and his generosity.

> Here is the list you asked for: two electric twits, a miniaturised fingernail-warmer, and a partridge in a pear tree.

Gentle separation is all you need here; the semicolon would have too heavy-handed an effect. But what happens if you need to add something to any item in one of those sentences? Can you still use a comma for that job? No:

Wrong

> Here is the list you asked for: two electric twits, both complete with flutter buttons, a miniaturised fingernail-warmer, and a partridge in a pear tree.

You've got a problem. Are the electric twits complete with flutter buttons, fingernail-warmers, and a bird up a tree? Presumably not; presumably the flutter buttons function only when they come with an electric twit and have nothing to do with the other items in the list. So a stronger separation is needed between the main items in the series, and the next step up the hierarchy is the semicolon:

> Here is the list you asked for: two electric twits, both complete with flutter buttons; a miniaturised fingernail-warmer; and a partridge in a pear tree.

61

The comma is now happily at work separating two items in a larger item, and the semicolon has swung into action as the main separator. Notice that the semicolon must continue throughout the list in order to give the same weight to each major item — don't make the elementary mistake of using the semicolon once and then reverting to the comma; preserve your hierarchy of meaning.

## The Semicolon as a Pivot

As you learned in Chapter 3, the semicolon is also used to separate control units, which are grammatically of equal rank and weight. A full stop can replace it with complete grammatical accuracy, but this heavier stop is inappropriate if the two control units are linked closely under the same general idea:

> The penalty for not turning work in on time is a lowered grade; the penalty for not turning it in at all is failure.

> The German defeat was already a fact before Berlin fell; Allied strategists, however, considered it vital that the city should be taken.

Both semicolons act as hinges between items which have a strong mutual relationship, even though they are complete as sentences should they wish to convert to the full stop. A semicolon is a pivot around which two control units pirouette in perfect balance.

# The Colon (:)

In past centuries the colon ranked between the semicolon and the full stop as something of a heavyweight. But those days are gone. It is still a heavier stop than the semicolon, but don't use it just for the sake of giving the full stop a rest. Its functions — there are two — are comparable to those of the single dash.

## The Colon Before Quotations

One function of the colon is to introduce quotations. It brings the sentence to a sudden, temporary halt and gives a cue for the quotation which is waiting in the wings. If the quotation is short, put it into quotation marks and carry on immediately after the colon: 'Some people seem to think that the colon's only meaning has something to do with the large intestine.' (Put the end stop inside the closing quotation mark if you are quoting a complete sentence, and outside if you are not. See also the section on End Stops, especially about the question mark, as well as the one on Quotation.) If the quotation is lengthy, do *not* use quotation marks; instead, give the quoted matter its own paragraph, missing a line before and after and indenting by five spaces — like this:

```
One of the interesting features of the
James Bond films is the presence of the
same kind of magic that has characterised
different products of our culture since
the days of Aladdin's Lamp and the Tales
of the Arabian Nights.  The magic may be
that of modern technology, as in Bond's
Aston Martin with the built-in ejector
seat, but it is magic all the same.
```

The colon is the ideal stop when a quotation is preceded by a full control unit of some length, or when a strong break is called for. But sometimes a quotation flows easily on from the words which introduce it, and the stopping power of the colon is too disruptive. Something gentler is needed:

So I said, 'Bring that Aston Martin over here!'

The colon wouldn't be wrong, but the gentler comma is more appropriate. It is also possible to omit the stop altogether:

Even the cliché, which can be defined as 'a worn-out phrase or situation', can still sometimes be appropriate.

It all depends on the flow of the sentence's meaning.


*The Colon as an Announcement Mark*

The colon is used most commonly to announce something important which is a direct result of what you have just written. The announcement can be a control unit or two, or it can take the form of a list of items:

It was quite clear to me that something had gone horribly wrong: the flutter buttons had been deliberately smashed, and the two biggest electric twits were pulsating and rumbling menacingly.

The boot of my car was big enough for everything: golf clubs, fishing rods, picnic basket, and my three biggest suitcases.

The colon, then, 'has acquired a special function: that of delivering the goods that have been invoiced in the preceding words'. This phrase, taken from Fowler's *Dictionary of Modern English Usage*, is itself an excellent example of the point it is making.

Sometimes the colon can be followed by a capital letter — the only stop, apart from the three end stops, which is entitled to this privilege — but only when the words which follow are even more separate than usual. Such is the case with a question:

You will probably have to answer some rather searching questions, such as this: Why do you think a tertiary department of English is justified?

## Exercise 7

Punctuate the following as a single sentence, using as middle stops the colon, semicolon, and comma.

Some famous writers have tried their hands at writing advertisements Lord Byron in the early nineteenth century Charles Lamb at about the same time Aldous Huxley writing in the middle of the twentieth century Ernest Hemingway Sherwood Anderson and William Faulkner all before the Second World War the list goes on and none of these major literary figures had more than minor success in writing an effective advertisement.

## The Dash (—)

Do *not* confuse the dash and the hyphen. The latter is a short line typed in the normal space between two words (*heavy-handed*), connecting them in meaning and telling the reader to think of them as a single word. The dash is a longer stroke denoting either a break in thought (in which case you use a single dash) or a digression (i.e., a parenthesis — in which case you use a dash pair). With handwriting there is no problem; you simply draw the dash with a slightly longer stroke than the hyphen. But typing methods vary. Many American typists use two hyphens for the dash, with no space on either side:

```
A parenthesis--and this is one--can be
typed with a pair of dashes.
```

But you may be more familiar with the space-hyphen-space method:

```
An equally good system is to space, type
a hyphen, and space again - which more
accurately simulates a break in thought,
and throws emphasis on the words after
the dash.
```

Use whichever method you prefer, but be consistent.

As a point of interest, you may see in older books that a dash has been printed with other middle punctuation before it, thus: , —. This is no longer the convention. Modern writers and printers use the dash on its own in order to maintain the stark abruptness intended.

For discussion of the single dash and the dash pair, see Chapters 2 and 3.

## Brackets (( ), [ ])

There are two main types: ( ) and [ ]. They are usually called brackets and square brackets respectively, although some call the curves *parentheses* and the squares *brackets*. Their uses are very clear: square brackets are usually reserved for the three editorial purposes explained below, while brackets are an alternative to the comma pair and the dash pair, and enclose a parenthetical remark (an aside).

The first purpose of square brackets is to tell your reader that the mistake in a quotation is not your own — that you are quoting material exactly as it appears in the source. This is how it works:

The letter came from Lisbon, the capitol [*sic*] of Portugal.

Lisbon, of course, is the *capital* of Portugal; the Latin word *sic* means here 'thus it appears', and is your defence against anyone who accuses you of a misspelling.

The second use of square brackets occurs when you quote material which needs brief clarification. For example, Oscar Wilde once wrote: 'I can resist anything except temptation.' But he wrote it in a play and gave the line to Lord Darlington, one of his characters:

> As Oscar Wilde wrote, 'I [Lord Darlington] can resist anything except temptation.'

In this case, your reader will naturally want to know who Lord Darlington is. If your context doesn't already explain this, satisfy curiosity in a footnote (the procedure for this is described later in this book).

The third use of square brackets involves ellipsis, i.e., omission. When you omit unnecessary words from a quotation and therefore use ellipses (three spaced full stops), you sometimes find that you have damaged the grammar of what you are quoting. Use square brackets to wallpaper discreetly over the crack:

> An eye-witness said of them: 'They wanted to amuse themselves at their guests' expense . . . [and] were vastly entertained by the antics of Sancho and the knight.'

These three are the only occasions on which you are likely to need square brackets.

Here are two additional points to remember about ordinary (curved) brackets. First, never put a middle stop just before the first half of the bracket pair; thoughts in brackets belong to the words just before, not just after, and no further separation is needed. Second, place end stops according to logic: if a parenthesis is part of a sentence, then the full stop comes *outside* the final bracket:

> It was the quickest way out (and the most dangerous).

But if you choose to bracket a whole sentence, remember that the end stop is *part* of the whole sentence, and that should be bracketed too:

> All writing has an intended audience. (Diaries and technical manuals are only possible exceptions to this.) Therefore, no writing can be judged good or bad outside the context of its intended reader.

It is quite possible for one complete sentence to contain another, encased in brackets. The bracketed sentence must then drop its initial capital letter and the full stop:

By the time he left Paris (the French Revolution was just beginning to hit its full stride), it was no longer a pleasant city to live in.

But such a sentence may at any time claim a question mark or an exclamation mark:

Some people who are fond of money (are there any who aren't?) have even tried printing it themselves.

The famous gourmet admitted that the reason he doesn't like peas (we shouldn't take him too seriously here!) is that they keep rolling off his knife.

When the outside sentence ends immediately after the bracket, the end stop must always be used whether the bracket contains an end stop or not:

It was the fastest car (but it was also the most dangerous!).

How can anyone not like lichen (apart from the problem of pronouncing it!)?

# 6 End Stops

There are only four ways of ending a sentence. You can choose a full stop, ellipses, a question mark, or an exclamation mark. Ellipses are not end stops, but it is convenient to treat them in the context of the full stop.

## The Full Stop (.)

In addition to its normal duty of ending a sentence, the full stop has two functions: to complete the action of ellipsis, and to point to abbreviations.

### The Full Stop in Ellipsis

Ellipsis is the act of omitting words in a quotation. To quote word-for-word from material which contains too many words is tedious, and may even distract your reader by offering him facts or ideas which are irrelevant to the topic. You must therefore omit the irrelevant parts, but you must discreetly tell the reader that you have done so. The easy way to do this is to use *ellipses* — three spaced full stops ( . . ) — to represent the words you have missed out. Both ellipses and omission can come at the beginning, in the middle, or at the end of a sentence, as we shall now see.

Suppose you want to quote only the latter part of this sentence, translated from Horace:

I, too, am indignant when the worthy Homer nods, but in a long work it is permissible to snatch a little sleep.

You do it this way:

. . . in a long work it is permissible to snatch a little sleep.

And suppose you want to omit the middle part of one of Macaulay's sentences on Machiavelli:

Such a display of wickedness, naked yet not ashamed, such cool, judicious, scientific atrocity, seemed rather to belong to a fiend than to the most depraved of men.

This is how:

Such a display of wickedness . . . seemed rather to belong to a fiend than to the most depraved of men.

Note that the punctuation of the original can also be omitted, if it makes the sentence grammatical as you quote it.

But ellipses should never ride rough-shod over a full stop. Let's say you want to quote the following two sentences except for the last support unit:

We shall not stop until the job is done. The men's morale is high, even though malaria is taking a murderous toll.

You therefore want to omit something *before* the end of a sentence, so you must put ellipses *before* the full stop:

We shall not stop until the job is done. The men's morale is high . . . .

And if you want to omit something *after* the end of a sentence, put ellipses *after* its full stop:

We shall not stop until the job is done. . . . even though malaria is taking a murderous toll.

It is worth mentioning here that good quotation is faithful not only to the original wording, but also to the author's attitude and intention. It is the easiest thing in the world to misrepresent a writer by quoting him out of context. To illustrate this point, I have chosen to misrepresent Macaulay's opinion of Machiavelli in one of the examples above. Macaulay's sentence was merely giving the views of many men towards Machiavelli, but his own views were very different. If I wish to be fair to both men, I must correct the impression I have given by explaining Macaulay's true opinion and by finding, if possible, another quotation to redress the balance. Perhaps this will do:

[Machiavelli was] a man whose public conduct was upright and honourable, whose views of morality, where they differed from those of the persons around him, seemed to have differed for the better . . . .

Misrepresentation is just as easy in ellipsis, so you must take great care that you are not suppressing any information which might be vital to a proper reading of the material you are quoting. Such an act would be an outrage against truth, as well as against an author. Consider this sentence, for example:

The king . . . agreed that his brother should be put to death.

Quite a barbarian, this king. But is this the full picture? Exactly what has been omitted from the sentence?

The king, *dreading what seemed the even worse alternative of plunging his country into bloody civil war, finally and in agony* agreed that his brother should be put to death.

We might still conclude that the king did wrong, but at least our moral judgement has the essential facts to go on. Ellipsis, in this example, would be a bad move.

There is a further use of ellipses, and we ought to cover it before passing on. Writers are fond of using them in their own style, sometimes to create a silence at the end of a sentence which they intend to sound ominous:

Traitors will be hanged, shot, and asked to leave the country. . . .

Avoid stylistic ellipsis, especially in critical essays. It is an expert's tool, and the amateur risks appearing adolescent.

## The Full Stop in Abbreviation

Stops in abbreviations sometimes cause trouble when they occur right at the end of a sentence. The best thing to do is also the easiest: use only one of the two stops unless there is a risk of confusion.

The word *brothers* will furnish an example. This word is sometimes abbreviated, as you know, in company names — *Carter Bros.*, for instance, is a firm run by two or more of the Carter brothers in partnership. (Note that this word is not abbreviated in normal writing: you do not say, 'My bros. and I'.) When the abbreviation comes last in a sentence, don't use the stop twice:

The town clerk decided to hire Carter Bros.

70

But other end stops might still be used:

You don't mean to hire Carter Bros.!
Are you really going to hire Carter Bros.?

With only the one stop used, though, confusion can still result:

Wrong

The building contract was won by Carter Bros. Builders, and other associated tradesmen, were keen to compete.

The reader has a bad moment here; it looks as if the second comma has committed the sin of separating a subject ('tradesmen') from its verb ('were keen to compete'). In fact, the sentence was intended as follows:

The building contract was won by Carter Bros.. Builders, and other associated tradesmen, were keen to compete.

The use of the full stop shows that a sentence has ended, and that 'Builders' is the first word of a new sentence, not the last word of the company title. Needless to say, the confusion isn't very much more irritating than the correction, and the best alternative is to rewrite the sentence altogether. It's easier to avoid a problem than to solve it. No such problem arises, by the way, with middle stops; they should be still be used, abbreviation or not:

I gave the contract to Carter Bros., but I think I may live to regret it.
He returned non-stop by air from the U.S.A.; I think he wishes he'd travelled by boat.

While we're on the subject of abbreviations, let's clear up a point which seems to puzzle some people. Our habit of ending an abbreviation with a stop (*Mr.* and *Mrs. and Dr.*) is so widespread that it might seem curious to see one sometimes without the stop (*Mr* and *Mrs* and *Dr*). The matter is quite without importance, but the reason may satisfy curiosity. There is a school of thought which omits the stop if the last letter of the abbreviation happens to be the last letter of the full word. Thus, *Doctor* ends with an *r* and so does *Dr;* therefore, a stop is unnecessary. The Australian Government Publishing Service *Style Manual for Authors, Editors and Printers* recommends this rule, so it is generally followed by Australian publishers.

# The Question Mark (?)

When you use a question mark, make sure that you are also using a question! And vice versa.

He asked who started the riot.

Who started the riot?

It's only too easy to put a question mark after a sentence which is not a question. The first example (above) contains a question, but it is not a question itself. The control unit is based on 'He asked', not on 'Did he ask . . .?'. There may be no problem with such a short group of words, but watch out for the longer ones.

A more understandable problem springs from the use of the question mark (or, indeed, any end stop) in the vicinity of quotation marks. Simplified, the doubt appears to start with this kind of situation:

Wrong

Did he say, 'Who started the riot?'?

The verb group ('Who started the riot?') is a question, and ought to conclude with a question mark before the close of quotation. But the control unit is based on 'Did he say . . .?' which is itself a question. Logically, therefore, a question mark is also required *outside* the quotation. But this looks peculiar, which is contrary to the intention of punctuation. One of the question marks ought to be sacrificed. Which one?

The ruling is based on priority. When the close of quotation coincides with the close of sentence, this is what you do:

(**a**) Put the end stop *outside* the last quotation mark if the quotation is *not* a complete sentence;
(**b**) Put the end stop *inside* the last quotation mark if the quotation *is* a complete sentence;
(**c**) But if the outside sentence is a question and the quotation is not, put the question mark outside the quotation marks. (This disqualifies rule **b**.)

This solves the problem we came across above, because 'Who started the riot?' is a complete sentence:

Did he say, 'Who started the riot?'
(*Rule* **b**)

It also solves this one:

Didn't he refer to the invention of the wheel as 'the greatest discovery since sliced bread'?
(*Rule* **a**)

And this:

Do you think this is fair: 'Student Guild fees are compulsory'?
(*Rule* **c** *in place of Rule* **b**)

See also the earlier section on the colon and the later one on quotation.

Perhaps it is timely to say a word on the device known as 'the rhetorical question'. This is a question asked by a speaker or writer when he obviously intends to answer it himself; one was used as the concluding sentence in the last paragraph but one. This is a perfectly acceptable device, but it is not without its danger. Asking a question calls for an answer, and your reader might give you one that you don't expect. Use the rhetorical question if it best suits your purpose, but use it as little as possible; and always hunt around for a more positive way of making your point.

# The Exclamation Mark (!)

Respectable advertising copywriters and journalists call this a 'shriek mark' or 'screamer'. If you want to cheapen your writing by being sensational or hysterical, then you can't do better than sprinkle the page liberally with exclamation marks. This isn't to say that you can't use the mark at all, but remember that discretion is the better part of exclamation. Admittedly, some great writers have peppered their pages with 'screamers' and got away with it, including a man from Stratford-on-Avon of no mean repute:

What a piece of work is man! How noble in reason! How infinite in faculty! In form and moving how express and admirable! In action how like an angel! In apprehension how like a god!

But we assume in our humility that we are not Shakespeares, and we tread his path with caution. If we are seeking emphasis, we can usually achieve it with words themselves and the order we put them in; that way, the exclamation mark has all the more impact when we do use it. But even when it does seem justified, is it really necessary?

> 'What are you going to be when you grow up?' asked his wife, nastily.
> 'Very funny,' the General replied.
> ['Very funny!' the General replied.]

If the above exchange is meant humorously, then the understating comma is drier than the sickly exclamation mark. Most people prefer their humour dry, not wet.

When you use the exclamation mark in conjunction with quotation marks, the rules are the same as those for the question mark. If the exclamation mark belongs clearly to the quotation, place it inside the closing quotation mark; if it does not, place it outside:

> He shouted, 'A pox on them both!'

> His ignorance was formidable. When he was asked who wrote *Don Quixote*, all he could say was 'Shakespeare'!

## Exercise 8

Write out the following sentences, inserting full stops, question marks and exclamation marks where necessary.

1 'These gates are locked to you' said the archangel.
2 He asked if we were going to apologise
3 Is he the one who keeps whistling 'Waltzing Matilda'
4 Is he ever going to stop calling out 'I'm rich I'm rich'
5 She asked me if I had been there before.
  'Never,' I replied.
  'Not even when you lived near by'
  'Not even then'
  'You must have led a very retired life'
6 D'you mean you've never seen *Oh, Calcutta!*
  (N.B. The exclamation mark belongs to the title.)
7 Ah, Harry And your friend Ichabod, too Why, what a tremendous surprise
8 She fled from the room in tears (and can anyone blame her)

9 (No, I didn't think you'd believe it. But I had to try)
10 With his most dazzling smile, he turned to me and
   murmured softly in my ear, 'Get lost'

# 7 Apostrophes and Hyphens

These two are neither middle stops nor end stops; they belong to individual words. They are not influenced by full stops, brackets, commas, dashes, or any other stop — in short, they have nothing to do with the structure or meaning of a sentence. But they *do* have something to do with the meaning of a *word* in the sentence.

## The Apostrophe (')

The apostrophe is a tombstone. It marks the graves of letters that have been squeezed out of a word, a process which takes place when two words are telescoped together to make another one — one which is easier to say. Thus, *do not* telescopes into *don't* and *will not* into *won't*, where the apostrophe waves forlornly in memory of the dead letters.

> **I'm** not going. I **couldn't** then, I **can't** now, and I **don't** think **I'll** ever be able to.

The bold-type words are contractions of others. Notice that the omission needn't be of only one letter; *cannot* drops *no* to become *can't*, and *I will* contracts to *I'll* by killing off *wi*. The apostrophe flies at a respectable half-mast over a mass grave as easily as over a single one. There are quite a few contractions such as these, but some of them have stopped bothering with the apostrophe: *bus, plane, photo* and *phone* have changed to their present state from *omnibus, aeroplane, photograph* and *telephone*. The original words are still used, though some not as commonly as others; but the transitions are rare these days: '*bus*, '*plane*, *photo*', '*phone*.

You can also use the apostrophe to indicate possession:

John's car; Perth's parks; a stone's throw; children's games; parents' permission.

But note two things. First, there is a difference between *the horses panicked* (*horses* just means 'more than one horse' and doesn't take the apostrophe) and *the horse's head* (where the 's means 'belonging to one horse'):

The horses head up into the hills.

The horse's head is caked with mud.

Second, there is a difference between *horse's head* and *horses' heads*; the first refers to one horse, the second to more than one. The placing of that apostrophe is very important. If you're still confused, try it this way: take the base-word on its own, and let the apostrophe and the *s* take care of themselves. Thus:

Your *car* has come. Here are your *car's* papers. [There's only one car.]

Your fleet of *cars* has arrived. Here are your *cars'* papers. [You've got a lot of cars.]

In the same way, *parent's permission* differs from *parents' permission*. In the first place, you cornered *one* of your parents to get what you wanted; in the second, you managed to out-talk both of them. The base-word is clear in each example. So it is, also, with the word *children*; it is already a plural word, so the only time an *s* can be added is to indicate belonging, and therefore goes after the apostrophe.

Be careful with the word *its*. If it's a contraction from *it is*, as the second word in this sentence is, then shove in the apostrophe. If it indicates belonging, don't:

*It's* a pterodactyl, but I can't find *its* nest.

*Its* is one of seven words, all indicating belonging, which do not use the apostrophe. You know them all: *my, your, his, her, its, our,* and *their*. (See the later section on Confusions for *its* and *your* and *whose*.) A last word on *its* — never, never write *its'*. There's no such animal.

You can also choose to use the apostrophe (or not) to form the plurals of figures:

the early 1900's, the early 1900s;
several size 16's, several size 16s.

The apostrophe is optional here.*

You *must* use the apostrophe, however, to form plurals or letters. See what happens when you don't:

Wrong

There are four ss and four is in *Mississippi*.

Thus the apostrophe is a sanity-keeper:

There are four s's and four i's in *Mississippi*.

For other plural possessives, vary the apostrophe-*s* formation according to sound. That is, avoid ugly *iziz* noises:

ladies' gloves, *not* ladieses' gloves;
the Jones's party, *not* the Joneses's party;
Moses' people, *not* Moses's people; but
Henry James's novels, *not* Henry James' novels.

Some of the words above can have too much *iziz* about them, but they can also have too little. Thus *the Jones' party*, if said aloud, sounds like a party thrown by *the Joans*; say *Jones's* (*Joansiz*) instead. Follow the sound-rule and you won't go wrong. The ordinary plural of *Jones*, by the way, is *Joneses:* 'The Joneses threw a party at the Jones's house.'

Next, use the apostrophe in memory of omitted letters if you deliberately write a passage of colloquial speech:

'An' Ah fink Ah'm a-goin' t'be sick,' he said.

Finally, don't let hyphenated words beat you.

Let's take father-in-law's car!
Did you hear that passer-by's comment?
I've asked you all here to tell me about your mothers-in-law.
What are your mothers-in-law's views about this company?

In the plural, add an *s* to the main word only; in the possessive, add an apostophe-*s* to the last word only.

---

* The Australian Government Publishing Service *Style Manual for Authors, Editors and Printers* recommends omitting the apostrophe here.

# The Hyphen (-)

A hyphen is a single short stroke squeezed into the normal space left between two words (*a three-bedroom home*). It joins up these words to show that they are to be read as one word; the physical joining is also a connection in meaning.

Be nice to the hyphen. It has been kicked around for years by people who get impatient with its exactness. It can certainly be overused; this book tries to do without it as much as it possibly can, almost to the extent of risking a misreading. But there are times when a word cries out for a hyphen. The word *misled*, for example, is sometimes read as *mizzled* instead of *mis-led*, even by people who ought to know better; yet *misled* is the dictionary-accepted spelling.

There is at least one use of the hyphen that cannot be challenged. If you are writing a word at the end of a line and you suddenly run out of space, break the word in two; put a hyphen at the end of the line; and then drop down to the next line for the second part of the word. There are likely to be examples of this on any page in almost any book. If possible, break the word at a point of emphasis; any good dictionary will show where this emphasis is. And *don't* put the hyphen at the beginning of a new line (a common mistake); the only punctuation allowed there are the dash, an opening bracket, and the capital letter. But although the use of the break-hyphen is acceptable, it is even more acceptable not to *have* to use it. Avoid breaking words in half at all times, even if you have to leave more white space at the end of a line than you're comfortable with.

And now for the twilight zone. Hyphens can be used to join two kinds of word: nouns and adjectives. By far the more common is the hyphenated adjective.

He is a well-known speaker.
She wore a grey-green skirt.
It was a never-to-be-forgotten speech.
It was a rollicking, rip-roaring,
here's-mud-in-your-eye kind of town.

These are all multi-word adjectives: a string of words all doing the job of one word in describing a noun. But notice that the same words can sometimes be used *without* the hyphen when they are *not* forming an adjective:

The speaker was well known.
The speech was never to be forgotten.
It was a well-planned attack.
*But* The attack was well planned.

It is a fairly safe guideline to assume that any multi-word adjective is likely to require hyphenation.

Multi-word nouns are a different matter. There is no point in hyphenating *mortgage broker*, *school teacher* or *meeting agenda*, because there is no possible clash of meaning. But *self-starter* and *mini-skirt* are hyphenated, just as most words beginning with *self* and *mini* (and *multi*) are hyphenated, and they will presumably retain the hyphen until usage wears it away and simply runs the original words together (*selfstarter, miniskirt*). Usage is the dictator here, and that is what makes certainty so difficult. Even the most up-to-date dictionaries are a little behind the times.

Some uses of the hyphen are clearer, though. When you add a prefix (such as *multi-*) to a word, hyphenate:

pre-Renaissance, anti-communist, ex-Prime Minister, post-Civil War, pro-Russian.

And hyphenation can make the difference between stolen goods and repair:

He recovered the chair.
He re-covered the chair.

Use hyphens to avoid awkwardnesses:

*Not* belllike *but* bell-like;
*not* recreate *but* re-create;
*not* a second hand grenade *but* a second hand-grenade *or* a second-hand grenade.

You should also use hyphens between the numbers twenty-one to ninety-nine:

thirty-two, fifty-five, one hundred and sixty-four, one thousand and ninety-six.

— and between fractions:

two-thirds, four-fifths, seven-sixteenths.

In other cases, use a hyphen only when not to do so might cause confusion or offer a different meaning from the one intended:

a drive in the country; a drive-in theatre.

Use the hyphen discreetly. Too many hyphens form a chain, which drags its clanking way across the page and sends the reader into a frenzy. But don't hesitate to use them, even in chains, if the result is clearer meaning or a deliberate effect of style.

## Exercise 9

Write out the following sentences, putting in hyphens and apostrophes where appropriate.

1 The policemans attitude had changed.
2 This is a for adults only book.
3 Four students have already given up our six week crash course.
4 The criminals record doesnt justify leniency.
5 Theyre interested in its flavour.
6 Its a clear case of insanity.
7 Hes a ninety kilo ex boxer and hes rarin to go.
8 You want to invent a one tooth comb for balding people? Now theres a world shaking idea.
9 She had a do that again and Ill kill you look in her eyes.
10 Do you mean a red winged beetle or a red winged beetle? (N.B. One comma is needed in this sentence.)

# 8 Agreements and Confusions

This chapter looks briefly at three points of grammatical agreement which are frequently misunderstood, and at twenty-three confused spellings and usages.

## *I* or *Me*?

The following four examples are all wrong in their use of *I* or *me*:

Wrong

He gave high marks to Jim and I.
How can you say that to a girl like I?
Can Professor Blenkinsop and me come in now?
Me and Pythagoras think you're the bee's knees.

One or two grammarians would like to give a belated respectability to sentences such as those, apparently out of a despair that the correct way will never be learned. This seems a pity, because the right way of using *I* and *me* is so easy — and there's hardly a rule in sight.

First, take the top example —

Wrong

He gave high marks to Jim and I.

— and mentally take out the other words in the same group:

Wrong

He gave high marks to . . . I.

There's no mistaking the mistake. Try it on the others:

How can you say that to . . . I?
Can . . . me come in now?
Me . . . think you're the bee's knees.

If a grammarian can accept that, he or she will accept anything. The same problem, and the same solution, applies to *us* against *we*:

Wrong

*Us* students must stick together.
It's too risky here for we life-savers.
Leave the brain-work to we computer-programmers.
*Us* conductors should stand up for our rights.

Keep trying that mental ellipsis; it never fails. Now for another point: 'Me and Pythagoras think you're the bee's knees' is wrong in another way. You always put the other person first:

Pythagoras and I . . . .

This isn't only good manners; it's good English. Cardinal Wolsey once infuriated his king, Henry VIII, by saying *'Ego et rex meus . . . '* ('I and my king . . .'). Good Latin, but awful diplomacy. The English language is spoken and jealously protected by many a latter-day Henry VIII, so be diplomatic.

# Verb-Subject Agreement

Each one of you*is* invited to take the examination. Every one of you *is* expected to pass.

*Each* and *every* are both singular; they go with *is*, not *are*. (But *they each have spoken* is right, because *each* is not the main word in the subject group.) The same applies to words such as these: *either, neither, anyone, everyone, everybody, nobody, none, no-one.*

This may seem a footling matter, but many errors in verb-subject agreement occur when the verb is separated by long distance from the main word in the subject group:

Wrong

Therisk of the workersare great.

The chief of the thousands of reformed alcoholics were too drunk to give his inaugural speech.

The word in each case, of course, is *is*. But don't be caught; the controlling words are sometimes near the end of the group, not the beginning. Such is the case with the words *of those people* in the verb group of the following sentence:

He is one of those people who are afraid to speak.

Apply logic. It rarely lets you down.

With collective words (singular words with plural meanings), verb agreement depends on the sense:

The government is happy with the budget.
*But* The government are arguing among themselves.

In the second example especially, the alternative would be most peculiar. Let common sense make the decision.

## Danglers

A 'dangler' is a word or a word-group, usually contained in a support unit, which fails to link up properly with the meaning of the control unit:

Wrong

*Having been damaged in the bows*, the captain struggled to get his ship back to harbour.

No doubt the captain did struggle; no man with damaged bows is likely to find things easy for a while. Surgery is required:

*His ship having been damaged in the bows*, the captain struggled to get his ship back to harbour.

The dangling end has been taken up and tied to the control unit, and the captain is no longer in pain. Here is a classic 'dangler':

Wrong

*Walking down the road*, the sky was blue.

A divine visitation, perhaps? That loose, dangling end needs tying up:

*As we were walking down the road*, we saw that the sky was
blue.

The effect of a dangling construction is not always
humorous, which is perhaps why the error is so frequent.

## Spelling Problems

> It's a damned poor mind that can think of only one way to
> spell a word.
> — U.S. President Andrew Jackson

Many people have difficulty in spelling properly, and the
main cause of their frustration is what they might call the
'illogicality' of English. This isn't quite fair. English is no
longer an entirely phonetic language, because pronunciation
has sometimes outstripped spelling; our words are almost
invariably logical in that there is a reason for almost every
non-phonetic spelling in the dictionary. We are dealing,
after all, with an old language; the early social history of
England was so turbulent, and the borrowings from other
linguistic families consequently so massive, that words which
look alike but sound different (and vice versa) often do so
because their origins are different in time and place.

All this is very well, but it doesn't help the poor speller.
The standard grammar books aren't much help, either; the
following example of a spelling rule is taken from one of
them, and is characteristic of them all:

> Where the final syllable of a word is stressed and has a single
> consonant after a single vowel, the consonant is doubled before
> a suffix beginning with a vowel.

There are at least seven different concepts or terms in that
sentence which the reader is expected to handle quickly and
to memorise for life, rather in the manner of a professional
juggler. As if that were not bad enough, the same book
then goes on to list four major exceptions which are
supposed to cover a hundred words or more.

These difficulties are enough, in themselves, to explain
why a thorough treatment of spelling is not attempted here.
Of the numerous words of advice which a poor speller can
be given, perhaps the most profitable is this: Buy a good
dictionary, refer to it constantly while proofreading essays,

letters, etc., and jot down troublesome words on the endpapers for easy reference. American dictionaries will list American spellings, of course, and you should come to a decision about whether to opt for American or English usage before you buy. Make sure in any case that the dictionary gives *etymologies* (the history of a word's meaning) for each word; as well as being an interesting study in itself, etymology is one of the surest ways to help fix a spelling in the mind. The dictionary you need is not cheap, but you are spending money in a good cause. If you are tempted to buy an inexpensive pocket dictionary, go ahead — but buy it as a *second* dictionary and carry it about with you in case of emergency.

## Word Confusions

One useful job this book can perform is the listing of a few of the more commonly misspelt or misused words. The list offered here, of course, is neither extensive nor comprehensive, but you might meet a few old friends.

### *Affect, Effect*

*Affect* is a verb and nothing but a verb:

> The heat *affects* me.
> He *affected* a dignified posture.

It means 'to influence' or 'to pretend to be or have'. *Effect* can also be a verb, but it means 'to produce or bring about':

> The government *effected* many changes.

Its other use is as a noun:

> The *effect* was powerful and long-lasting.

### *Aggravate*

This means 'to make worse', not 'to annoy'.

> His headache was *aggravated* by the heat and the flies.

### *Aitch*

This may look like a sneeze-noise, but it is the way the

letter *h* is spelled — and pronounced. There's no such word as *haitch*.

## All right, Alright

The first is correct. *Alright* is not accepted as good English; avoid it. If you have any doubts, remember that the opposite of *alright* must logically be *alwrong*, which is all wrong.

## Allusion, Delusion, Illusion

An *allusion* is a reference to something:

He made an *allusion* to my book.

The other two are similar in meaning in most uses ('an error, a misconception'); they may differ in certain cases. *To delude* means 'to deceive', while *to illude* means 'to trick'. Perhaps the clearest difference between them is illustrated best by this:

It was nothing but a stage *illusion*.
He has *delusions* of grandeur.

## Among, Between

*Between* implies *between the two*; *among* implies more than two. But *between* is used when several individual elements are being treated:

The difference *between* the three essays is really very slight.

## Complementary, Complimentary

The first means 'completing':

The second lecture is *complementary* to the first.

The second means 'flattering':

He was most *complimentary* about my green hair.

## Could of, Could have

The first is incorrect. Perhaps the frequency of the fault might indicate an unawareness of verb constructions.

## e.g.

*Exempli gratia* is Latin for 'for example'. Put in the two abbreviation stops (to prevent your reader from wondering what an eg is) and treat it exactly as you would treat 'for example' — which almost invariably should have a comma on both sides unless it begins or ends a sentence, in which event it has a comma on only one side. Use this abbreviation only to list examples; do not use it as an automatic replacement of 'for example'.

## etc.

The Latin *et cetera* (or *et ceteri*) means 'and the others'. Punctuate as for *e.g.*, above. Avoid it when you can, because it is an easy way out of thinking up more relevant arguments or examples. And don't say *etc., etc.*; this is equivalent to saying 'and the others, and the others'.

## Different from, Different than

Use the first.

## i.e.

This is from the Latin *id est*, 'that is'. Again, treat this abbreviation as you would treat *e.g.*, above.

## Irregardless

This one seems to be gaining in popularity. Don't you mean *regardless*?

## Its, it's

*Its* is a possessive word:

Give the horse *its* head!

*It's* is a contraction of 'it is':

*It's* that man again.

Never put *its'* — it doesn't exist logically.

## Lay, Lie

*Lie* means 'to tell a tale' or 'to lie down'.
*Lay* means 'to lay a thing down'.

I think I'll go and *lie* down. (NOT *lay* down.)

## Literally

This usually means 'strict adherence to the letter', or 'meant exactly'. Thus, if someone tells you 'Your dog kennel is *literally* knee-deep in fleas!', then your dog has problems.

## Orient, Orientate

These are two of the most notorious victims of overuse. The original meaning was 'to face the east' or 'to get one's bearings', but the recent trend gives it the added twist, for both words, of 'designed for', 'meant for', or 'suitable for'. Thus we are likely to hear of *a peace-oriented mission* instead of the simpler *a mission for peace*. The belief seems to be that the trendier version booms with importance, but the boom is that of a hollow log. The tendency is getting worse; I am daily expecting to hear *this apple is eating-oriented*.

## Principal, Principle

The first means 'chief' (the *Principal* of the school; the *principal* speaker); the second means 'a basic truth' (an ethical *principle*; a *principle* of engineering).

## Stationary, Stationery

The first means 'stopped, fixed'; the second means 'writing paper, envelopes':

The car was *stationary*.
She wrote to me on scented *stationery*.

## Their, There, They're

*Their* is a possessive word (*their* clothes); *there* is a word of place (over *there*); and *they're* is the contraction of *they are*.

## Unique

It means 'one only'. *That desk is unique* means that there is no other desk like it. *Almost unique* is acceptable if there are only two or three other similar items, but *rather unique* or *fairly unique* are self-contradictory.

## Whose, Who's

*Whose* is a possessive word (*whose* hat?); *who's* is the contraction of *who is* (*who's* coming?).

## Your, You're

The first is a possessive word (*your* hat); the second is the contraction of *you are* (*you're* crazy!).

# 9 How to Present an Essay

The tactics of writing an analytical essay are discussed in Chapter 4. The present chapter offers advice on how to present such an essay to the teacher or reader. Specifically, it treats basic guidelines, methods of quotation, systems of reference and bibliography, some publishers' abbreviations, and plagiarism.

Many of the methods listed here are taken or adapted from *The MLA Style Sheet*, a booklet on essay format produced by the Modern Language Association of America. Not everyone agrees with all the *Style Sheet*'s recommendations, but it is one of the most widely followed such guides in English and should be consulted for fuller explanations and suggestions. The teacher or reader may, of course, have additional requirements of his own.

## Guidelines

1 **Please type your essays.** Impeccable handwriting is rare; typewriters are not. On the other hand, your teacher will prefer good writing to bad typing. Decide which you're better at, and do it. If you're equally bad at either, you'll find it easier to improve your typing. If you must write, use ink, not pencil.
2 **Keep a carbon copy of your work.** Teachers, alas, are fallible creatures, and a legible copy is your safeguard against loss or destruction caused by a tutor who has just seen your thirty-seventh spelling error in as many lines.
3 **Type on one side of the paper.** This doubles the number of sheets of paper, but it greatly reduces the time and frustration needed to flop the essay over and back again

every time the reader comes to the foot of a page. Furthermore, the continual sight of beckoning white paper is too great a temptation for some tutors, who will pepper your work with suggestions and comments you might not otherwise have got.

4 **Typing should be double-spaced; so should large handwriting.** Apart from being easier to read (and don't underestimate your tutor's gratitude here), double-spaced typing makes on-the-spot comments far less cramped and far more easily pinpointed.

5 **But type longer quotations single-spaced.** (See item 13 below.)

6 **Face your essay with a cover sheet.** Give your own name and your tutor's, the subject (Philosophy 10, Mathematics 112, Literature 213, etc.), the title of the paper, and the date due. The title needn't be repeated on the first sheet of the essay.

7 **Leave a left-hand margin of at least an inch and a half, and a one-inch margin on the other three sides.** This leaves room for local comments.

8 **Attach all sheets together in the top left corner with a staple or a paper-clip.** Use a staple if your essay features footnotes; but if you have provided endnotes, use a paper-clip so that the endnote sheet can easily be detached. Take care when stapling that you don't ram the metal through any words; if you've attended to item 7, of course, this problem shouldn't arise.

9 **Provide notes and a bibliography (see later) when required.**

10 **Underline titles of separately published works.** Underlining represents italics, which are used for the names of books, long poems, magazines, journals, films, and even ships. Reserve quotation marks for works *not* published separately: articles in magazines, short poems, lectures from a symposium, book chapters, etc. Underlining distinguishes a book instantly from a book chapter or article. It is common, but not compulsory, to underline only the words and not the spaces between them, on the principle that it is difficult to italicise a space. For example: A Phoenix Too Frequent; The Tree of Man; The Common Sense of Science. Titles of journals and their accepted abbreviations — e.g., The

<u>Times</u> <u>Literary</u> <u>Supplement</u> <u>(TLS)</u>; <u>Australian</u> <u>Literary</u> <u>Studies</u> <u>(ALS)</u> — should also be underlined, as should words or phrases which are distinctly foreign (<u>leitmotif</u>; <u>sine</u> <u>qua</u> <u>non</u>; <u>tour</u> <u>de</u> <u>force</u>). Underline for emphasis only if you have to; your natural style should be capable, usually, of showing emphasis by rhythm or syntax.

11 **Use quotation marks around works which have not been published separately,** as mentioned in item 10. End stops imposed by you should go outside the closing quotation mark.

12 **Put shorter quotations in quotation marks and incorporate them within your normal text.** A 'shorter' quotation consists of fewer than about twenty words, or, in poetry, two lines or less. Since the division of lines is important in poetry, mark it with a shilling stroke ( / ) thus: 'Season of mists and mellow fruitfulness, / Close bosom friend of the maturing sun'.

13 **Set longer quotations apart from your normal text.** A 'longer' quotation consists of more than about twenty words of prose or more than two lines of poetry. Give it its own paragraph, as follows:

```
Miss a line before you quote, and indent
five spaces (about an inch) from the left
margin.  Single-space your typing so that
the lines of the quotation snuggle together;
this, in concert with the indentation and
the missed line before and after, makes the
quotation stand out on the page.
```

14 **Number the pages clearly, in the top centre or top right.** Pagination begins with the first sheet of the essay, not with the cover sheet.

15 **Proofread!** Check for punctuation, words missed out, typing and spelling errors, accurate quotations, acknowledgment of sources, broken continuity of thought, ludicrous statements, and so on. The more mistakes you pick up, the fewer your tutor can fault. If you're brave enough, ask your worst enemy to glance through the essay in search of errors. He or she will find them.

```
NAME:      Malcolm Pennicuick
COURSE:    B.A. English
SUBJECT:   Literature 313
TITLE:     'The Quest Tradition in
           J.R.R. Tolkien's The Two
           Towers'
TUTOR:     Dr V.M.Page
DATE DUE:  3 November 1976
```

# Methods of Quotation

Some points are already dealt with under 'Guidelines' and 'The Colon Before Quotations'; refer to 'The Question Mark' for matters concerning the placement of stops inside and outside quotation marks.

## *Quotation Marks*

Quotation marks, like brackets and Siamese twins, come in pairs. It doesn't matter whether you use single or double quotation marks so long as you are consistent:

Wrong
'I'm inconsistent," he said.
"I can see that,' replied the hypocrite.

But single and double marks can be used together when one quotation contains another:

'He yelled "Thief!" as I left the shop,' said John.

If you are writing dialogue, you will need to know certain conventions. First, put a *comma inside* the quotation marks after a quoted sentence when the speaker comes after:

'Go away,' said the Bishop.

But put the comma after the speaker when he comes first, and end the quoted sentence with the normal end stop *inside* the quotation marks:

> The Knight stared and said, 'No, I won't.'

The two other end stops take priority whether the speaker comes first or last:

> 'What's up with him?' said the Castle, puzzled. Giggling, the leading black Pawn said, 'He's had a tiff with the White Queen again!'

And when the speaker interrupts the quotation, put a comma after the speaker and re-open the quotation with a small letter —

> 'Be quiet, you vicious little rumour-monger,' snarled the Bishop, 'or I'll bash you on the head with this mitre.'

— unless, of course, the quotation was broken at the end of a sentence; in that case, put a comma to mark the end of the dialogue sentence, put a full stop after the speaker, and re-open the quotation with a capital letter:

> 'Pawn to Queen's Bishop four,' announced the Black King. 'Look lively, you lot, or we'll be late for tea.'

These are the dialogue printing conventions you will find in most books. They differ slightly from the methods of punctuating a quotation in a critical essay; the reason for the difference is in the different purposes of each. In dialogue, the emphasis is on what the speaker has to say, which of course is printed *inside* the quotation marks; therefore, all punctuation is attracted inside as well. In a critical essay, however, the emphasis is very much on what *you* have to say, and the quotation is secondary; thus, punctuation is attracted *outside*. It is a hair-fine point, but the logic is quite clear. (See the sections on the colon and the question mark for more comments on the placement of punctuation with quotation marks.)

## Longer Quotations

As you know, quotations of more than about twenty words are set apart from the body of the essay so that they are easier to read; they miss a line above and below, they are single-spaced, and they are indented five spaces from the left. You also know that they are usually introduced by a colon. This section deals with five variations of punctuation which will help you to slip in and out of a quotation with ease.

First, the colon can announce a quotation which begins with a capital letter and ends with a full stop:

> One of the purposes of quotation is to reproduce the original as nearly as possible. If you wish to start quoting after the original sentence has begun, it is unnecessary to use ellipses (. . .); just begin with the lower-case letter of the word you want to begin with, unless its first letter happens to be a capital. If the quotation ends with a full stop, and you intend to begin your own next sentence anew, let the full stop stand — like this.

The take-up sentence (this is it) then begins with a capital letter. Now, if you want to continue your sentence after the quotation has finished, you should treat the quotation as a kind of parenthesis, beginning with the colon and closing with the dash:

> Both the colon and the dash belong, in this case, to the leave-off sentence above and the take-up sentence which follows the quotation. Needless to say, this is the only occasion when such a deformed parenthesis is justified! Note also that if the quotation ends in the source with an end stop, that end stop may be omitted since the quotation is already in parentheses. This is optional, though, and such omission is usually only a matter of taste

— all of which means that you maintain your own grammatical continuity at the expense of a parenthetical interruption. If you do decide to leave out that full stop, by the way, try to make sure that the quotation is short — much shorter than the example.

That was the second variation. The third is exactly the same except that the parenthesis now consists of a pair of dashes —

> The dash pair emphasises that the quotation is a brief interruption, meaning that the end stop may be omitted and that the take-up sentence will resume the sense of the leave-off sentence

— which allows you to enforce what you are saying in the strongest way with a minimum of fuss. In both this variation and the one before, of course, the take-up sentence begins with a small letter, not a capital.

The fourth variation uses ellipses after the quotation, a technique designed to tell the reader that you have stopped quoting before the end of the original sentence:

> In a quotation of this kind, of course, you would put the end stop after the ellipses only if the take-up sentence is a new one. . . .

This take-up sentence, as it happens, *is* a new one.

The fifth variation dispenses with the colon, or any other announcement mark, altogether. Its use is still optional, but the omission slides you and your reader swiftly into the quotation. This swiftness may be defined as

> a shock tactic. It lets you begin the quotation in the middle of the sentence without ellipses, but you must always ensure that the transition from your grammar into that of the quotation is smooth and total.

This variation is not common; nor should it be. Its greater impact should be nursed, ready for the great occasion when it is justified. Overuse will blunt its edge.

It is usual to acknowledge the source of a quotation by a reference adjacent to the quotation, or perhaps by a numbered note. See the following section for details of how this might affect punctuation.

## References

There are three ways of acknowledging the source of a quotation or reference: by a very brief comment in the body of the text, by a numbered footnote, and by a numbered endnote. The first of these is easier, neater, and cleaner; use it whenever you can. The choice between the other two is a matter for you and your teacher.

The purpose of a reference is to provide the reader with as much information as he needs to go to your source himself. This information usually includes the following: author's name, title of publication, place of publication, name of publisher, date of publication, and the page

***Fig. 5***   *Book entries in notes and bibliography*

**Formula:**

Note:   [1]A.N. Author, <u>Title Underlined</u> (Place: Publisher, year), p. 32.

Bib.:   Author, A.N. <u>Title Underlined</u>. Place: Publisher, year. (In bibliography, indent five spaces for each line after the first.)

**Examples:**

One Author

Note:   [2]Leonard Woolf, <u>Beginning Again</u> (London: Hogarth Press, 1964), p. 185.

Bib.:   Woolf, Leonard. <u>Beginning Again</u>. London: Hogarth Press, 1964.

Two Authors

Note:   [3]Walter E. Houghton and G. Robert Stange, <u>Victorian Poetry and Poetics</u> (Cambridge, Mass.: Harvard University Press, 1959), p. 27.

Bib.:   Houghton, Walter E., and Stange, G. Robert. <u>Victorian Poetry and Poetics</u>. Cambridge, Mass.: Harvard University Press, 1959.

Three Authors

Note:   [4]Bernard R. Berelson, Paul F. Lazarsfeld, and William N. McPhee, <u>Voting</u> (Chicago: University of Chicago Press, 1954), pp. 93–103.

Bib.:   Berelson, Bernard R., Lazarsfel, Paul F., and McPhee, William N. <u>Voting</u>. Chicago: University of Chicago Press, 1954.

number. You do not need to give all these details every time you make reference to the same book or article; you can often get away with just the author's name and the page number (e.g., **Smith, p. 97**), provided that you have given a full reference in an earlier acknowledgment.

More Than Three Authors

Note: [5]Albert J. Reiss, Jr., et al., Occupations and Social Status (New York: Free Press of Glencoe, 1961), p. 9.

Bib.: Reiss, Albert J., Jr., et al. Occupations and Social Status. New York: Free Press of Glencoe, 1961.

Author and Translator (or Editor)

Note: [6]Ivar Lissner, The Living Past, trans. J. Maxwell Brownjohn (New York: G.P. Putnam's Sons, 1957), p. 68.

Bib.: Lissner, Ivar. The Living Past. Trans. by J. Maxwell Brownjohn. New York: G.P. Putnam's Sons, 1957.

[*For an editor, substitute* ed. *for* trans.]

Editor instead of Author

Note: [7]J.N.D. Anderson, ed., The World's Religions (London: Inter-Varsity Fellowship, 1950), p. 143.

Bib.: Anderson, J.N.D., ed. The World's Religions. London: Inter-Varsity Fellowship, 1950.

Collection: Part-Author with Editor

Note: [8]Paul Tillich, 'Being and Love', in Moral Principles of Action, ed. Ruth N. Anshen (New York: Harper and Bros., 1952), p. 663.

Bib.: Tillich, Paul. 'Being and Love'. Moral Principles of Action. Ed. By R.N. Anshen. New York: Harper and Bros., 1952.

[Adapted from Kate L. Turabian, *A Manual for Writers of Term Papers, Theses, and Dissertations* (London: University of Chicago Press, 1969), pp. 73–76.]

*Adjacent Reference*

When the reference required is very short, it is utterly pointless to go to the trouble of making a footnote or endnote, especially as it may irritate the reader — whose irritation will increase if all he finds in the footnote is a page reference. If it is already clear which book you are discussing, all you need to do is put the page number in brackets at a convenient place in the sentence (p. 16), or after the quotation itself:

> The 1973 printing of *The MLA Style Sheet* has this to say: 'Information given in your text need not be repeated in a footnote; hence many notes can easily be shortened or avoided by taking the trouble to give *complete* titles or dates or names of authors in the text itself' (p. 16.)

The quotation is a complete sentence, so the full stop goes inside the quotation mark; the page number is then given in brackets which also enclose a full stop. If the quotation had stopped short of the end of the sentence, it would have been given ellipses: '. . . in the text itself . . .' (p. 16). The full stop then encloses everything and marks the end of your own sentence. A neater method is to avoid ellipses, however: '. . . in the text itself' (p. 16). It is then clear that you have omitted the last part of the original sentence; the full stop marks the end of your own sentence and encloses everything inside it.

If you are quoting from a play, perhaps one by Shakespeare, quote the appropriate lines and then give the reference immediately afterwards, also in brackets:

> O, then my best blood turn
> To an infected jelly, and my name
> Be yoked with his that did betray the best!
> (*The Winter's Tale,* I.ii)

Those numbers refer to Act I, scene ii. Line numbers have been omitted here because the play runs to many editions and the line numbers differ. If you are using a specific edition of the play and have said so in an earlier note (as well as in the bibliography — see later), it is sensible to give the line numbers too. A reference to Act IV, scene iii, lines 13 to 23 would be shown thus: (IV.iii. 13–23). Notice, by the way, that Act numbers are upper-case Roman (I, II, etc.), scene numbers are lower-case Roman (iii, iv, etc.), and line or page numbers are Arabic (5, 6, etc.). Separate them with full stops.

The great advantage of adjacent reference, then, is that

the reader can absorb brief, but important, information in a second or two; he doesn't have to interrupt his reading to chase a footnote number to the foot of the page, or an endnote number to the end of the essay.

*Fig. 6*   *Article entries in notes and bibliography*

---

**Formula:**

Note:   [1]A. Writer, 'Article Quoted', <u>Journal</u> <u>Underlined</u>, volume number (Month, year), 105.

Bib.:   Writer, A. 'Article Quoted'. <u>Journal</u> <u>Underlined</u>, volume number (Month, year), 103–9.

(In bibliography, indent five spaces for each line after the first. Note that journal pages are not designated *p. or pp.*, and that the bibliography entry for articles, unlike that for books, lists page references: all the pages of a book are deemed to have been consulted, but all those of a journal are obviously not.)

**Examples:**

Journal Article

Note:   [2]Barbara K. Varley, 'Socialisation in Social Work Education', <u>Social Work</u>, VIII (July, 1963), 105.

Bib.:   Varley, Barbara K. 'Socialisation in Social Work Education'. <u>Social Work</u>, VIII (July, 1963), 103–9.

Magazine Article

Note:   [3]S.L.A. Marshall, 'The Fight at Monkey', <u>Harper's Magazine</u>, November, 1966, pp. 111–22.

Bib.:   Marshall, S.L.A. 'The Fight at Monkey'. <u>Harper's Magazine</u>, November, 1966, pp. 111–22.

Encyclopaedia: Signed Article

Note:   [4]J.W. Comyns-Carr, 'Blake, William', <u>Encyclopaedia Britannica</u>, 11th ed., IV, 36–38.

Bib.:   Comyns-Carr, J.W. 'Blake, William'. <u>Encyclopaedia Britannica</u>. 11th ed. Vol. IV.

---

Encyclopaedia: Unsigned Article

Note:    [5]'Sitting Bull', <u>Encyclopaedia</u> <u>Americana</u>, 1962,
         XXV, 48.
Bib.:    'Sitting Bull'. <u>Encyclopaedia</u> <u>Americana</u>. 1962.
         Vol. XXV.

[Adapted from Kate L. Turabian, *A Manual for Writers of Term Papers, Theses, and Dissertations* (London: University of Chicago Press, 1969), pp. 78–9.]

## Footnotes

Sometimes, adjacent reference is difficult; a full note is required to give full information. Begin by typing a *superior* number (i.e., one that stands above the line) immediately after the material quoted or referred to; if the material is followed by punctuation, put the number after every punctuation mark except the dash, and space before you type the next word.[1] The number is then repeated at the foot of the page and followed by the note.[2]

The footnote is handy enough, because the eye can travel fairly quickly between the number and the note; it is not as handy as an adjacent reference, which puts the reader to no bother at all, but it has access to more space and therefore allows fuller information to be given. Lengthy notes are not encouraged: some writers use the footnote as an excuse to write mini-essays commenting on some point which they feel can't appropriately be discussed in the text. If it can't be appropriately discussed, then don't discuss it. If you feel the matter to be of some importance, you can always open an appendix and tuck it discreetly away at the end of the essay; but such methods are pretentious unless the essay is part of a book.

The first full reference to a text is best made in a note, all references to it thereafter offering only the author's name and the page number, or perhaps only the title and the page number. What you offer depends on what you

---

[1] Place a footnote as this has been placed. Leave space at the foot of the page and type ten underline-spaces (or draw a short line) from the left. Miss a line and type the number. Drop down another half-line, space, and type the note. Just as you would for a longer quotation, single-space the lines.

[2] Numbers should be unadorned — no full stop, no oblique (/), and no brackets.

need to offer; if you use the author's name in your text, and the author has written more than one book, it might be necessary only to note the *title* and page number. Common sense is the best guide. In the first reference, it is a good idea to add a comment such as 'All future references to the book will be made to this edition', or 'All quotations from the poem are taken from this edition', etc.

Perhaps the easiest system of numbering footnotes throughout the essay is to do so consecutively; that is, start with the number 1 and keep going. If you prefer, you can re-start the numbering for each page which carries footnotes — thus two notes on page one would be numbered 1 and 2, and five notes on page seven would be numbered 1 to 5.

## Endnotes

You will have seen books which carry what appear to be footnote numbers without carrying footnotes. The numbers relate to notes which appear at the end of the chapter or article and have a page to themselves. Endnote numbers are, of course, consecutive; there is only one number 1, only one number 7, and so on.

The disadvantage of the system, obviously, lies in the extreme separation of the notes from the text. This can be overcome by allowing the reader to detach the endnotes page (which is, surprisingly, headed **Endnotes**) and place it beside the essay for quick reference. If you write essays with endnotes, therefore, hold them together with paper-clips, not staples.

The great advantage of endnotes is equally obvious: there is no desperate guessing or minute calculation as the bottom of the sheet comes remorselessly through the typewriter. In this, at least, endnotes are far easier to handle than footnotes. Furthermore, endnotes preserve the clean look of the page; it is sometimes tedious to read an essay which trickles tortuously through a maze of footnotes.

## Bibliography

The bibliography is your final list of texts consulted and used in the essay. It is additional to footnotes and endnotes, and is arranged alphabetically by authors' surnames. There are several methods of presenting a bibliography, and your

Department may have specific requirements of its own. If not, the following system, based partly on *The MLA Style Sheet* and partly on Kate Turabian's *A Manual for Writers of Theses, Term Papers, and Dissertations* (London: University of Chicago Press, 1969), is probably comprehensive enough for your present needs.

Perhaps it is appropriate first to list the main differences between an entry in a bibliography and an entry in a note:

| **Bibliography** | **Note** |
|---|---|
| 1 Full information given about author, title, date and place of publication, edition, etc. | 1 Apart from the first full reference, information is that which is immediately relevant to context. |
| 2 Alphabetically listed by authors' surnames. | 2 Sequentially listed; no alphabetisation. |
| 3 Surname followed by comma followed by initials. | 3 Where name used, initials or first name followed by surname. |
| 4 No page reference (unless to specify part of journal consulted). | 4 Frequently carries page reference. |
| 5 No commentary. | 5 Commentary as desirable. |
| 6 Uses mainly full stops to give each element parity with the others. | 6 Uses commas, brackets and colon, chiefly to allow it to be read as a sentence. |

Refer to Figs. 5 and 6 for examples of entries in notes and bibliography.

## *Some publishers' abbreviations*

These are just a few of the standard abbreviations used in footnotes, etc., to save time and space in printing. They are listed (on page 106) primarily to help you understand them when you come across them in books and articles. Be wary of those which are asterisked if you intend using this list in writing your own essays; some are beyond your likely needs, and others are superfluous or even replaceable (*et al.*, for instance, might be in the process of being displaced by the straightforward 'and others').

104

***Fig. 7**   Sample of an essay's bibliography page*

BIBLIOGRAPHY

Anderson, J.N.D., ed. The World's Religions.
London:  Inter-Varsity Fellowship, 1950.

Comyns-Carr, J.W. 'Blake, William'.
Encyclopaedia Britannica.  11th Ed.
Vol. IV.

Houghton, Walter E., and Stange, G.Robert.
Victorian Poetry and Poetics.
Cambridge, Mass.:  Harvard University
Press, 1959.

Lissner, Ivar.  The Living Past.  Trans.by
J.M. Brownjohn. New York:  G.P. Putnam's
Sons,1957.

Marshall, S.L.A. 'The Fight at Monkey'.
Harper's Magazine, November, 1966,
pp. 111-22.

Reiss, Albert J., Jr., et al.  Occupations
and Social Status.  New York:  Free
Press Glencoe, 1961.

Tillich, Paul. 'Being and Love'.  Moral
Principles of Action.  Ed. by Ruth N.
Anshen:  New York:  Harper and Bros.,
1952.

Varley, Barbara K. 'Socialisation in Social
Work Education'.  Social Work, VIII
(July, 1963), 103-9.

Woolf, Leonard.  Beginning Again. London:
Hogarth Press, 1964.

c., or ca. (Latin *circa*) — about. (E.g., ca. 1976.)
cf. (Latin *confer*) — compare.
*cf. ante* — compare above.
*cf. post* — compare below.
e.g. (Latin *exempli gratia*) — for example.
ed. (plural, edd.) — edition.
ed. (plural, eds.) — editor or edited.
*et al.* (Latin *et alii*) — and the others.
*et seq.* (Latin *et sequens*; plural, *et seqq.*) — and the following.
*f. (plural, ff.) — and the following. (E.g., page 4ff).
i.e. (Latin *id est*) — that is.
*ibid.* (Latin *ibidem*) — in the same place.
l. (Plural, ll.) — line. (E.g., l. 10; ll. 10–13.)
*loc. cit.* (Latin *loco citato*) — in the place already cited.
MS (plural, MSS) — manuscript.
n. (plural, nn.) — note. (E.g., nn. 5 and 9.)
n.d. — no date.
n.n. — no name.
n.p. — no place (or no publisher).
no. (plural, nos.) — number.
*op. cit.* (Latin, *opere citato*) — *in the work already cited.*
p. (plural, pp.) — page.
*passim* (Latin; sometimes *et passim*) — here and there.
q.v. (Latin; *quod vide*) — which see. (E.g.: 'This applies to Smith's article (q.v.) as well as this one.')
rpt. — reprinted.
rev. — revised, revision.
*sic* (Latin) — thus; i.e., thus it appears in the original.
trans. — translated, translator.

## Plagiarism

A plagiarist is one who takes for his own unacknowledged use the thoughts or writings of another person, thereby claiming them as his own. Plagiarism, in short, is downright theft.

Certain universities and other tertiary establishments suspend a plagiarist from his studies the moment he is

---

* For *ibid.*, *loc. cit.* and *op. cit.*, prefer the simpler practice of putting author or title followed by page number; e.g., Kitto, p. 16 **or** *The Greeks*, p. 16.

detected. If this seems a little severe, consider that plagiarism is illegal and that the punishment might therefore be much worse.

The School of English at the Western Australian Institute of Technology acts against a plagiarist as follows:

> A person caught plagiarising the first time may expect to receive a mark of O for the assignment concerned; a second offence will lead to a similar mark for the subject as a whole, and the culprit will be asked to leave the class.
>
> (Extract from notes distributed to first-year students)

As you see, plagiarism is taken seriously.

There may be some difficulty in deciding what constitutes plagiarism and what does not. The following examples should help; they are taken from Porter Perrin's *Handbook of Current English* (Glenview, Illinois: Scott, Foresman and Company, 1968).

The original source is taken from Lionel Trilling, 'F. Scott Fitzgerald', in *The Liberal Imagination*.

> Thus, *The Great Gatsby* has its interest as a record of contemporary manners, but this might only have served to date it, did not Fitzgerald take the given moment of history as something more than a mere circumstance, did he not, in the manner of the great French novelists of the nineteenth century, seize the given moment as a moral fact. . . . For Gatsby, divided between power and dream, comes inevitably to stand for America itself.

## Plagiarism

```
Of course, the one thing that makes The
Great Gatsby interesting is its picture
of the life of the twenties, but if that
were all it would be out of date. Instead,
like the great French novelists, Fitzgerald
made the particular moment a moral symbol.
Gatsby, the main character, divided between
power and dream, represents the American
dilemma.
```

Apart from 'divided between power and dream', our plagiarist makes no direct quotation from Professor Trilling. But the ideas are indisputably stolen. Note that plagiarism is often easy to detect because of the difference between the ideas and the general style, and because of lapses in thinking — such as this plagiarist's self-contradiction between the first sentence and the last.

*Fair Paraphrase*

> As Lionel Trilling points out, <u>The Great Gatsby</u> is much more than a record of the manners of the twenties. In miniature, Gatsby represents America, 'divided between power and dream'.[1]

Don't bother looking for the footnote — it is clearly going to acknowledge Trilling's article and book. This paraphrase is considered fair, partly because of the willingness to footnote the source, and partly because of the courteous acknowledgment of Trilling's name in the first sentence.

The message, then, is clear. Always acknowledge your sources, either in the text or in a note (or both), and put other people's words into quotation marks or into an indented paragraph. Due acknowledgment is essential; your essay will then be judged, as it should be, on how well you make use of your sources in your essay's argument.

# 10 Self-Test

The effectiveness of punctuation tests is dubious. Even if you score highly, your result doesn't necessarily mean that you can punctuate: it might only mean that you can work under test conditions. The justification of such tests, however, is that they are valuable exercises in proofreading. If you can proofread well, many of your problems are over.

Part of the purpose of the *Survival Kit* is to emphasise that a sentence may be technically correct without conveying the intended meaning. It can be right if the meaning is *x*, but wrong if the meaning is *y*. This is why the first ten questions contain an (a) sentence and a (b) sentence; the first is guaranteed correct, and you are asked to check that the second yields the same meaning. If it doesn't, it is wrong — even if it seems technically correct. This basis of comparison is not provided for the other thirty questions, which are correct or incorrect in their own right.

Answers are printed after the test. These are sometimes absolute and sometimes commentatorial. I hope, therefore, that the test will be a useful exercise in reading and understanding, either for the individual or for class discussion.

Be on the lookout for Word Confusions (see pages 86–90) as well as points of punctuation. Bear in mind also that not all the questions need correction — but that a sentence may contain one, two, three, or even four errors. So look before you leap.

In scoring the test, be as severe on yourself as you can. In a compound word requiring three hyphens, for instance, deduct a mark for every hyphen you omit. (But don't let severity overcome common sense — deduct *one* mark for a *pair* of commas, not two.) In short, count a mark lost for every error you make. If you make more than thirty, you haven't read this book properly; more than twenty, and you could use some revision; between ten and twenty, and you're not quite up to scratch; around half a dozen, and you're good; none at all, and you can write your own *Survival Kit*. Take no notice of how much time you needed to finish the test; speed is useless without accuracy. As a rough guideline, though, I might mention that most candidates in such tests as this seem to take between forty minutes and an hour.

## Instructions

Proofread these 40 questions. For the first 10, mark the (b) sentences wrong if they do not mean the same as their (a) sentences. Pencil your suggested corrections in the book, or write out the revised sentences for yourself. After you are satisfied that you can do no more, turn up the Answers (on page 112) and total your errors.

1 (a) The meeting approved the plans of the committee.
  (b) The committees' plans, were approved by the meeting.

2 (a) Dr Malibu (the chief medical officer) bought some envelopes and notepaper.
  (b) Dr Malibu, the chief medical officer bought some stationary.

3 (a) The Press always reports the activities of the President's wife and daughters.
  (b) The President's daughter's activities, are always reported by the Press, so are those of his wife.

4 (a) If you keep thinking about it, a big problem sometimes gets bigger.
  (b) The trouble with a big problem is it's habit of getting bigger. When you think about it.

5 (a) People should be punished if they are dishonest.
  (b) People, who are dishonest, should be punished.

6 (a) But the Prime Minister argued the point.
  (b) However the Prime Minister argued the point.

7 (a) Although he felt depressed, by the time he reached Rottnest Island he had decided to buy that boat of yours.

(b) Although he felt depressed by the time he reached Rottnest Island, he had decided to buy youre boat.

8 (a) The instructor asked who was next.

(b) 'Whose next'? asked the instructor.

9 (a) They worried about the effect the plans they made would have on the audience.

(b) 'We're worried in case our plans effect the audience and they're attitude,' they said.

10 (a) Politicians are paid by the people and should serve the needs of the people.

(b) Politicians, who are paid by the people, should serve the needs of the people.

11 *Lord Sandwich*: Pon my honour Wilkes, I don't know whether you'll die on the gallows or of the pox.

12 *John Wilkes*: That must depend My Lord upon whether I first embrace Your Lordship's principals or Your Lordship's mistresses.

13 The case held very little; two books, which were torn; a broken binder; a pair of cracked glasses, and an ill used fountain pen.

14 Nobody in the strip club heard him, (there minds were on other things).

15 'Alright, Einstein, whats the answer'?

16 'I dont believe it,' said the new midshipman. 'I always thought a sextant, was a navel deviant.'

17 The cook told him and me to peel the potatoes.

18 Tennessee Williams' recent play does not however, indicate much difference in his view of the world.

19 Our happy go lucky sergeant just did'nt care: he never bothered to clean his rifle, and his wig smelled.

20 His fingers moved deftly, no one stirred the air was electric.

21 Isaac Newton often called the father of modern science was one of those men whose most famous ideas have been popularised into distortion.

22 Carlyle said, that the true university of his day, was a collection of books.

23 Lambs frolic and gamble over the body of a dead lion.

24 I hope your not thinking of going alone Jane, said Tarzan stroking his chimpanzee.

25      The universities and colleges representatives attended none of them believed that things were as bad as they seemed.

26      He wouldn't accept the initial offer the salary wasnt high enough for his day to day expenses.

27      'Now I can sing every word of 'Sarie Marais!' " she cried excitedly.

28      Never use a comma, which isn't necessary.

29      Most over the counter remedies don't guarantee success, some of them may even be useless.

30      And Noah he often said to his wife when he sat down to dine, 'I don't care where the water goes if it doesn't get into the wine."

31      He came to W.A.I.T., parked his car, went to the Bookshop, and, when told for the fifteenth time that his main text book had still not arrived, proceeded quietly and systematically to tear page thirty six out of every book in the shop.

32      To quote from Heller's novel 'Catch-22'; 'Some men are born mediocre, some men achieve mediocrity, and some men have mediocrity thrust upon them. With Major Major it had been all three.

33      They wanted you and I to attend the lecture.

34      One of his characteristic plays on words was this: 'The length of a person's life often depends on the liver.'

35      At first it seemed to be the usual kind of essay, however, their emerged unusual problems when he began to delve.

36      Illness poverty eccentricity these were the causes of his ruin.

37      He spoke on several matters. Each of which were irrelevant to the advertised subject.

38      By absorbing this information, the student can see exactly, what future assessment will entail.

39      'When its eight o clock, she said, 'please take my brontosaurus for its' walk'.

40      The principle reason for his defeat was his habit of antagonising the many open minded voters.

## Answers

1 There is only one committee — therefore 's, not s'.

Also, the comma drives a wedge between the subject group and verb group in the control unit: omit it.

2 Put a comma after *officer*, thus completing the comma pair to match the (a) sentence's brackets. Otherwise, the (b) sentence becomes a remark addressed to Dr Malibu. Also, *stationary* should be *stationery*.

3 The word is *daughters'*, not *daughter's*; the President has more than one. Remove the intruding comma between subject and verb groups (*activities are*), and strengthen the second comma into a semicolon or a full stop. This second comma is sometimes called a comma *splice* — it splices, or joins, two word groups which must be kept apart. The comma is the only middle stop which cannot be used to connect two sentences. See Chapter 3.

4 *It's* should be *its*. *When you think about it* is a sentence fragment; the question is whether or not a fragment is justified here. The trouble stems from that troublesome *it* in the (a) sentence: does it refer to *a big problem*, or to what happens in general when you think about a problem? The evidence seems strongly in favour of the first alternative; so omit the full stop, cut the capital letter down to size, and incorporate the fragment into the subject group. (Moral: Take great care with the word *it*.)

5 Delete the comma pair. *People should be punished*, which is the meaning of the (b) sentence, is certainly not the meaning of the (a) sentence.

6 Put a comma after *However*. Otherwise the words become a sentence fragment, which does not have the sanction of the (a) sentence.

7 The (b) sentence is technically correct; but it does not carry the same meaning as the (a) sentence, which places the depression before the journey began. The (b) sentence implies that the depression might have resulted *from* the journey. Therefore, put the comma back in its first position. Also, *youre* is wrong. No, don't bother putting in the apostrophe; the word is possessive and must be *your*.

8 In the same way, *whose* is confused with *who's* — the contracted form of *who is*. And the question mark belongs to the question, which is *inside* the quotation marks.

9 *Effect* is confused with *affect*, and *they're* with *their*.

10 The sentence is correct. Both 10a and 10b say the same thing: that politicians are paid by the people, and that politicians should serve the needs of the people. (Compare the correct use of the comma pair here with the incorrect use in question 5.)

11 This famous anecdote has been abused here in two ways. *Pon* is the abbreviation of *upon*, and an apostrophe must be hired to mourn the dead *u*: *'Pon*. And *Wilkes* is a form of address in this sentence, therefore requiring punctuation fore and aft (*honour, Wilkes, I*). There is no need for quotation marks in this or the next question, as the dialogue is in the conventional printed format of a play.

12 *My Lord* is also a form of address here and needs its commas on both sides. Also, change *principals* to *principles*. I realise that *principals* might be justified as meaning 'representatives' or, just possibly, 'employers'; but this does not adequately explain the reference to the gallows. The other half of Wilkes's barb is aimed at the company Sandwich keeps; this half is aimed at the peer's beliefs.

13 *The case held very little*, followed as it is by a description of what it did hold, clearly calls for an announcement mark; change the semicolon to a colon (the dash will do at a pinch). Since one of the items described is listed with a comma, the separation of all the items must be performed by a semicolon series. Therefore, convert the final comma to a semicolon. Don't forget to hyphenate *ill-used* as a compound adjective. A hyphen in *fountain pen* is fussy; as a rule, compound nouns are easier to see than compound adjectives.

14 Never put a comma before a bracket. And where is the sentence's full stop? It is lurking inside the brackets. Dig it out and make it do its job, outside. Finally, change *there* to *their*.

15 *Alright* is a cuckoo in the nest of *all right*: drop it over the side. *Whats* doesn't exist; it is the contraction of *what is* and needs an apostrophe before the *s*. The question mark belongs inside the quotation marks.

16 *Dont* should be *don't*. The comma after *sextant* is a burglar breaking into the control unit: throw it out.

Correcting *navel* to *naval* completes the maritime aspect of this excruciating pun, but it loses the sexuality. Act according to your sense of humour.

17 The sentence is correct. Blot out *him and* and see.

18 *However* is a signpost word. Add a comma in front.

19 Hyphenate *happy-go-lucky*. *Did'nt* should be *didn't*.

20 Replace the comma splice with a full stop or a semicolon. *No one stirred the air was electric* are two fused sentences; mend by the same means as for the comma splice. As for *no one*: to hyphenate or not to hyphenate? Either is fine; sticklers put it in, progressives leave it out.

21 There are three acceptable versions:

(i) Isaac Newton, often called the father of modern science, was one of those men ... .

(ii) Isaac Newton, often called the Father of modern science, was one of those men ... .

(iii) Isaac Newton, often called 'The Father of Modern Science', was one of those men ... .

In each version, the comma pair is interchangeable with a pair of brackets or dashes. The capitalisation can be reduced according to taste, and the quotation marks, if they are felt necessary in the first place, can restrict themselves to *father*.

22 Remove those burgling commas.

23 The word is *gambol*. What you think of the personal habits of lambs is beside the point.

24 This is how to do it: 'I hope you're not thinking of going alone, Jane,' said Tarzan, stroking his chimpanzee.

25 This is what you should have:

The universities' and colleges' representatives attended.
None of them believed that things were as bad as they seemed.

There are several universities and colleges here. If representatives had been sent by only one college and one university, the words would have been *university's and college's representatives*. A semicolon after *attended* is unjustified, as there is no real connection between the two sentences.

26 Put apostrophes into *wouldn't* and *wasn't*; use two hyphens in the compound adjective *day-to-day*. (Note that the hyphens aren't necessary if a word isn't a

compound adjective: 'He came here from *day to day*.')
De-fuse the two sentences by using a full stop or, more
appropriately, a semicolon, colon, or dash. You can also
use *for* preceded by a comma. (See Chapter 3.)

27 First, make those quotation marks consistent: if you
open with a single mark, close with one. In this case,
simply reverse the closing single and double marks.
Second, pull the exclamation mark away from the title
(it doesn't belong there, although you probably didn't
know that) and put it between the double and single
closing quotation marks — in other words, logically
enough, make it the end stop of the exclamation.

28 The comma in *Never use a comma, which isn't necessary*
isn't necessary. In fact it's downright wrong — it says
that commas are never necessary. The sentence's
meaning and punctuation are delightfully in conflict, and
demonstrate once again why a control unit does not
encourage single middle stops.

29 Hyphenate *over-the-counter*. Avoid the comma splice by
erecting a stronger barrier: full stop, semicolon, etc.

30 If you open with a single quotation mark, you must end
with one. Chesterton's use of both *Noah* and *he* smacks
of redundancy, and you are technically justified in
striking out *he* or in putting a comma after *Noah* to
effect a conversational introduction. To do so would
spoil the fine balance of the line, however.

31 The only thing wrong with this sentence is the missing
hyphen in *thirty-six* (all numbers between twenty-one
and ninety-nine are hyphenated). All the commas are
right because all the word groups are dominated by the
single word *he*; they are therefore *multiple* verb groups
within the same control unit, and a comma series is as
strong a separation as you need. This is a more
complicated sentence than any dealt with in this book,
but its principle is so easy to grasp that its inclusion here
seemed appropriate. A final point: the comma after *and* is
unnecessary but correct (see Chapter 3, 'End Note').

32 Since it is a separate publication, *Catch-22* should be
underlined (i.e., italicised), not quoted. A comma after
*novel* is a natural emphasis for the title, but it risks the
implication that *Catch-22* is Heller's only novel. Knock

out the semicolon in favour of the colon. Restore the closing quotation mark.

33 Blank out the *you and*, and the mistake glares.

34 The sentence is correct.

35 Mend the comma splice with a semicolon or full stop. Substitute *there* for *their*.

36 There are several possibilities:

(i) Illness, poverty, eccentricity. These were the causes of his ruin.

(ii) Illness, poverty, eccentricity: these were the causes of his ruin.

(iii) Illness; poverty; eccentricity; these were the causes of his ruin.

(iv) Illness. Poverty. Eccentricity. These were the causes of his ruin.

The first and second versions are best. Semicolons are too clumsy for such light duties, and full stops (an attempt at a stylish sentence-fragment series) are stretching the point. The colon may be replaced by a dash, and the full stop in the first version by a semicolon.

37 This is not a justifiable sentence fragment; replace the full stop with a comma. Change *were* to *was* to agree with *each*.

38 Omit the comma after *exactly* — it mauls the insides of the control unit. If you wish to emphasise *exactly* (but why?), then that comma is not the way to do it: underline instead.

39 This is the way it should be: 'When it's eight o'clock,' she said, 'please take my brontosaurus for its walk.'

40 Again, *principle* is confused with *principal*. And don't forget that hyphen in *open-minded*.